Er ¹

You've probably hear̶c̶ ...̶c̶ nappens," and it certainly happens to some people harder than others. Rick is that man. I've known Rick since he was a teenager, and I'm confident you'll quickly be drawn into his extraordinary story of tragedy, failure, and personal loss. Yet, his example of faith to *dream again* is the real story here. It's something we all need to learn.

—Dave Divine, Pastor, The Church at Chapelhill

Rick tells a unique story of nearly unspeakable pain and loss. However, his story also simultaneously retells the story of everyone who ever experienced the crushing loss of a close family member or the humiliation of a public "failure." Rick's story will connect your heart to one of the few universal collective human realities and will plant this undeniably magnificent seed of truth: you can dream again—if you embrace the art of surrender.

—Pastor Terry Yancey, District Supt., AGK

Having known Rick since we were kids at church camp and then again in Bible college, I never would have imagined the tragedy his future would hold. When we reconnected decades later, I heard his story for the first time and was inspired by what God had done through terrible circumstances. If you feel low, Rick has been lower. If you need a lift, this is the book for you.

—Allen White, Author of *Exponential Groups*

I have had the privilege of hearing Rick's story over the last few years. I have heard it on long bicycle rides on country roads, on trips from Carlinville, Illinois, to the Brass Door Restaurant in Carrollton, and at many sit-down lunches we have had over the years. Just when I think *How much more can a man take?* he would tell me another part of his life that would cause my heart to ache with his. Rick's story says that Jesus is alive and well in us today! Jesus promised never to leave us, and that truth is incredibly evident in Rick's story!

—Rev. Dayton Poe, Wheat State Retreat Director

When Jesus said, "In this world you will have trouble," it turns out He wasn't kidding. Whether self-inflicted or random, we've all faced difficulties of living in a broken world. Rick Unruh tells a story of pain, loss, and failure that only a few can identify with, but also a story of restoration that all can be encouraged through. He tells the story well because it's his own. His story and God's restoration will inspire you to *dream again* in spite of whatever life has thrown your way.

—Greg Perkins, Director of Church Health and Men's Ministry, Southern Missouri

Self-Surrender:
THE KEY TO
Dreaming
AGAIN

Self-Surrender:
THE KEY TO
Dreaming
AGAIN

RICK UNRUH

REDEMPTION PRESS

Published by Redemption Press, PO Box 427, Enumclaw, WA 98022
Toll-Free (844) 2REDEEM (273-3336)

Redemption Press is honored to present this title in partnership with the author. The views expressed or implied in this work are those of the author. Redemption Press provides our imprint seal representing design excellence, creative content and high quality production.

ISBN 13: 978-1-68314-910-1 (Print)
978-1-68314-911-8 (ePub)
978-1-68314-912-5 (Mobi)
Library of Congress Catalog Card Number: LCCN 2019906692

Dedication

THIS BOOK IS DEDICATED TO OUR SON, LANDON, we will never forget you. We only shared 12 years with you, but you left a lasting impression on so many. You brought such great joy and laughter to our world, yet you also had this sensitive side that was aware when people were having a bad day and just needed to have an arm put around them. One of my favorite memories is you sitting on the porch with your arm around mom after a bad day and my favorite picture is of you walking beside your mom, with your arm around her.

To my wife, Tamela, when we said for better or worse, it's hard to imagine the "worse" that we have seen together, yet I love you more today than I ever have and I am more thankful than ever for God's gift and to have you by my side in our journey.

To Dake & Darian. So much I could say, but so little space. To see how well you both have turned out, despite the devastating blow you had to deal with. It would have been easy to quit. But you both are thriving in life and in your careers, makes us so proud to be your parents. Having three boys taught us so much about love and what an amazing gift from God you are. You both are an inspiration to your Mother and me. We love you!

To our wonderful daughter-in-law's, Kristi and Taylor. So many great qualities that you both have, but let's cut to the chase, nothing greater than having daughters-in-law that love our sons, unconditionally. We are blessed. We love you both!

Sadie, Londyn, Tate, & our future grandchildren, because we are believing for more! You light up our world, and in the pain of our loss, you are a great reminder of the joy in life.

To my dad, Loren. You have been a rock, many a day I just wanted to give up; you always found the right words to say. Your steadfastness is a powerful trait that has carried you through every trial in life, including the loss of your wife and the tragic loss of your grandson. Your faith in God has always been steadfast.

To my Mother, who is in heaven, you didn't just talk about faith, but lived it out, even in your greatest pain. Little did you know that when you were writing in your journal during your battle, that it would become a part of my book over 32 years later. That you helped write the closing chapter in a way only you could.

To my in-laws. You gave me the greatest gift I have ever had, your daughter and the love of my life. You have always been there for us, and so grateful for your love and encouragement.

To all Landon's friends, teammates, classmates; The list seems endless of the people we need to thank for your love and support. We have been blessed to be surrounded by so many great people. Thank You!

Contents

Foreword 11

CHAPTER 1: Physical Surrender 13

CHAPTER 2: Fifteen Flat Tires 19

CHAPTER 3: Transformation 31

CHAPTER 4: Blindsided 37

CHAPTER 5: Cracker Jack Prize? 41

CHAPTER 6: The Unmerry Christmas 51

CHAPTER 7: Life Goes On 61

CHAPTER 8: The Early Years 71

CHAPTER 9: "Your House Is on Fire!" 83

CHAPTER 10: Takotsubo: Broken Heart 87

CHAPTER 11: Triggers 97

CHAPTER 12: Healing through Coaching 105

CHAPTER 13: The Dedication 111

CHAPTER 14: The Pursuit of Happiness 115

CHAPTER 15: Roadside Encounter with God 121

CHAPTER 16: The FBI 133

CHAPTER 17: God Sent Jack 151

CHAPTER 18: The Power of Comfort 157

CHAPTER 19: 45 Hamburgers to Go............................ 167

CHAPTER 20: Feels like Christmas Morning 173

CHAPTER 21: Work Diet... 179

CHAPTER 22: Roses—in Prison?................................ 187

CHAPTER 23: Takotsubo Strikes Again....................... 193

CHAPTER 24: The Lonely Holidays............................. 199

CHAPTER 25: The Greatest Hamburger Ever!............. 201

CHAPTER 26: Time Served 205

CHAPTER 27: $887 Parking Spot............................... 211

CHAPTER 28: Self-Surrender 223

CHAPTER 30: The Storm.. 233

CHAPTER 31: Dream Again.. 237

Closing 245

Foreword

YOU OFTEN HEAR STORIES about an individual life, and you think to yourself, *Seriously?* When you look at the life of Rick Unruh, your mind immediately begins to ask, *What next?*

Rick has been my friend for many years. Over thirty years ago, I served as a counselor at a youth camp. Each of those young men were special, but that year there was one young man I knew God had a plan for. Rick Unruh and I became lasting friends. Being lasting friends is something totally different than just friends. Lasting friends walk through the storms together and come out on the other side better for being friends.

Rick has experienced loss that I would not wish on my greatest enemy. Yet, during the loss, Rick has always had the ability to come back. I have watched over the years and wondered to myself, *Is this going to be the one that takes Rick out of the game of life?* He comes back, smiling and believing that God has a plan and future for him.

As you take the time to read Rick's story, I want to remind you of a few things. First, God is the only one who can determine when you are finished. It does not matter how many times you are attacked; God is the one who determines your future and your completion.

Second, hold on to nothing tightly. When you think that you have it all and you see that God has blessed you greatly, that seems to be what gets attacked. Rick has lost the most precious treasures in life, yet he still has what matters most.

Third, remember who is on your team. When life throws you a curveball and you feel that you are finished, remember that there is a team behind you that will help you win the game.

My joy has simply been watching from the outfield as Rick has gone up to bat time and time again. Strikes were thrown, he has swung, and at times I thought he was out. The good news is that there was a team behind him that helped to keep the game going.

My greatest prayer as you read this book is that you will not cry for Rick but dream again as Rick has done. You are not out; you are not finished. God has a plan, and no matter what happens, you will be back in the game and victory will be yours.

Dr. Billy Thomas
Senior Director, US MAPS

CHAPTER 1

Physical Surrender

THIS TRIP WASN'T JUST A BUMP IN THE ROAD; it felt more like the termination of all my dreams. I was officially finished. God could never use me now. I would forever be labeled a felon. I was an embarrassment to my family, my friends, my church, my Bible college—and the list could go on and on.

God's plan for my life had just been washed into a river that flows into an ocean of one disappointment after another.

After years of searching and preparing for my purpose, the Dream Again Counseling Center launched. I felt as if I had finally been lifted from the pits of despair after our family's tragic loss. My life had found a purpose once again. I felt alive.

This blow felt like I had just been knocked out in a championship bout, and now I was left desolate, defeated, and crippled from the blow. It was over—the final countdown had begun.

I had grown up in a loving, Christian home with a long heritage of godly examples. I had been called to the ministry at a young age and had always tried to live my life on the straight-and-narrow path.

Over the next few hours, I said goodbye to my family and to my freedom. My hope that this was just a bad dream dissipated with each mile marker that we passed.

There was some chatter, but everyone was avoiding the

elephant in the car. We were all doing our best to mask our fear of the unknown. How was this going to impact our lives forever?

Questions were running rampant through my mind. How did I end up in this mess? *How much more can my family handle? Why, God?* How could God ever use someone as broken as me? *I am a complete failure.* I was drowning in a sea of self-pity, with no lifeline anywhere in sight.

Six weeks before this day, I had entered the courtroom as a defendant and stood before a federal judge. The federal prosecutors were asking for thirty- to thirty-six months; through the grace of God, I was only sentenced to fifteen months in federal prison for my involvement in a mortgage-consulting group. I was ordered to self-surrender on March 22, 2010.

We arrived at Yankton, South Dakota, and checked into a motel the night before I was to self-surrender. Sleep was elusive that night, as my soul crawled back into the cave of despair and hopelessness. This was my last night with my wife, Tamela. We had been married twenty-three years. How was she going to survive? How was my youngest son, Darian, going to handle his senior year of high school without his dad? *All his baseball games I am going to be missing. The birthdays. The holidays.* How would my oldest son, Dake, deal with all this as he was launching into his new career and moving to Kansas City? So many unanswered questions, so many unknown fears. *When is enough, enough? I want to be strong, but I'm just not sure that I can be.*

That night also brought back memories of the fateful day when we had lost our twelve-year-old son, Landon. The loss of a child makes you feel like your own life has ended. But you hold on to your remaining family tightly. And now, I was going to be separated from the one thing that held us together—each other. From the pit of despair, our family had somehow rallied together, and we were climbing ever so slowly upward again. About the time it appeared we had our life back on track, we were leveled with the devastating news of the investigation and eventual prison sentence.

Now, I just wanted to quit. Life had become too over-whelming—too many losses, too many failures. *The embar-rassment and shame of going to prison, the never-ending grief of losing our son, and now I am going to be separated from my family—the driving force, the reasons to keep liv-ing. How much is one person supposed to take?* I tossed and turned all night.

The next morning, we parked our car in front of Yankton Federal Prison Camp (FPC) and made our final walk together as we crossed the street to the control center where I was to check myself in and say my last goodbyes. We crossed the street in silence, observing every little detail of my home for the next eleven and a half months. The fear and dread of the separation I was about to experience was welling up inside, and I was trembling

We walked through the doors of the control center, and I said a sentence that I had no idea would become prophetic words on my journey in Yankton: "I'm Rick Unruh, and I'm here to self-surrender." There was no way I could compre-hend what those words would eventually mean to me over the course of the next year, as God began a powerful work in my life. I would come to understand their true meaning and would learn to fully "self-surrender."

Felon. This will become my new label, a constant reminder of my past. I was walking into a physical prison, but I was already living in a spiritual prison of shame, regret, and deep hurt.

And yet I would find freedom in prison. Freedom from the shackles of our grief and the burdens of my failures. Only when I was willing to surrender "self"—all my hurts, all my pain, all my regrets, and all my questions—and just trust that I genuinely began to understand freedom.

Prison has a way of slowing life down, with few distractions and much less of the busyness of life that often gets in the way of us hearing from God. Romans 8:28 says, "And we know that for those who love God all things work together for good, for those who are called according to his purpose." But here is one of the key misconceptions about this verse, in my opinion: it doesn't say that all things that happen to us *are* good. The word "all" encompasses the good and the bad. "All things"—even bad, horrific things in our lives—God takes these and *works them together* for the good. How could something good come out of losing a child or a parent, a house burning down, a financial crisis, or spending time in prison?

These are brutal things to go through, and on those days in my life, it seemed especially hard to grasp Romans 8:28 as a truth. All I could feel was the pain of that day. But in the end, God was going to take those events to mold me, shape me, and give me a testimony to bless others.

But I couldn't see any of that yet. That first day at Yankton FPC, the officer I surrendered to instructed me to say good-bye to my family. One last hug and kiss, and they left the premises. The officer waited for them to get out of sight; she didn't want them to see me getting patted down and taken away. As they walked away, I plastered a fake smile on my face as they silently stepped out the door and disappeared. It was official: I was in custody, a federal prisoner. *This is it, the beginning of the end of my life.*

My thoughts start churning wildly: *This is my new reality. What will prison be like? Is it really like what you see on TV? What about gangs? How will I stay safe? What if I sit at the wrong table? What are all the unwritten rules?*

The Enemy loves to wreak havoc in our minds with the fear of the unknown. Fear screams the worst possible scenarios, but only faith can calm the screaming lies of the Enemy.

I walked into R & D (receiving and discharge), where

I was officially registered into the system. I felt numb and dazed. After another pat down (and a much more thorough one, I might add), I traded in my street clothes for my prison uniform—khaki pants and a khaki shirt.

This book traverses the twists and turns of my journey—from my family heritage and the loss of my mother, to ministry, to drifting, to the loss of my son, to prison, and ultimately to God opening up the ministry door to dream again.

It is Tamela's and my prayer that this book exemplifies God's love and plan for your life even when you have taken a wrong turn that leads to circumstances that leave you feeling helpless. Knowing that when you trust Him, you can truly dream again and fulfill God's plan for your life.

CHAPTER 2

Fifteen Flat Tires

IT HAD BEEN A HOT SUMMER NIGHT, and a light breeze was blowing through the open windows on my grandfather's farm in Kansas. The breeze made things just bearable. It was around 5 a.m. when I was startled out of a deep sleep to noises coming from the kitchen. The aroma of bacon drifted into my room, along with the sizzling of the cast-iron skillet. Grandma was fixing breakfast.

On a farm, the days start early to get everything accomplished. While most farmers eat their breakfast and hit the ground running, my grandfather was a dedicated Christian, and his days never started without honoring God first.

As a young boy, I often opted to skip breakfast to grab a few more minutes of sleep before the long day, only to be awakened later by the loud voice of my grandpa as he knelt at the couch and cried out to God. I never remember him missing a day. I listened to him list each one family member by name and pray for their needs and protection; he prayed for the crops, the farm, the church—and the list went on and on.

My great-great-grandfather was part of a community of Mennonites who had left Russia (Ukraine) in 1874 to pursue their American Dream of becoming landowners and finding religious freedom. Several of them found their way to Great Bend, Kansas, to set up their homestead, including my grandfather's ancestors.

They faced death several times while on the boat coming to America. Here is one of those instances, recorded in the diary of their leader, Tobias Unruh:

> May 21. Windy, stormy in the evening and all through the night. The ship rocked back and forth, dishes fell and broke to pieces. It was a terrible night and appeared as though we would perish. Many thought the sea would be our grave.

> May 22. Storm continued. Great waves were thrown against the ship. Water was a foot deep on deck. I, with Peter: "Lord save us." True, the hand of God was watching over us.

> It's hard to imagine, but if that storm had been victorious, I would not be here today. But God sees all things and had a plan for my family.

Some of the group met with President Ulysses S. Grant:

> Tobias writes on August 8. We left New York 8 a.m. to see the president. At 8 p.m. we were introduced to the president in his residence. He is the president of all the states of the union of the United States. Our agent Hillers sent his servants to him with a message and also our petition and plea. He looked them over and then requested that we come and meet him. He was a plain man and very friendly. He informed us of the Constitution has a concession that it will not override a man's conscience and religious freedom is guaranteed. He appreciated this information and expressed our gratitude and bid him Adieu. He then offered us his hand and gave us a very warm friendly goodbye. We then returned our hotel.

Later a member of the Mennonite community wrote a summary of the diary. "He who has prompted her forefathers to forsake their comfortable homes and flee from the country of Ukraine where chaos and ruin would rule, that led them to the land of liberty and freedom, He said, 'I am with you always, even into the end of the world.'"

My great-grandfather's homestead was just a few miles outside of Great Bend.

We heard many stories of the early hardships of living on the homestead. We also heard some stories that were probably exaggerated a little. Like the one my dad, Loren, loves to tell, of having to walk several miles in two feet of snow—all uphill—to get to school and then back home—again, all uphill—now in three feet of snow.

During my dad's growing-up years, the work on the farm never ended and depended heavily upon the boys pulling their fair share. Life for them, as for so many during that time, revolved around work, school, and church. Even amid the farm's demands, my grandfather made sure they were at church every time the doors were opened. He understood hard work, but he also recognized the importance of attending worship services and his spiritual impact helped define his legacy.

I was blessed with a heritage that was instrumental in starting a church in Great Bend. My grandfather and two of his sisters donated the land and then helped build it. It was a heritage to be passed on and it sent eight people in our family into full-time ministry as pastors and missionaries.

My father always loved sports but was never allowed to play because of the demands on the farm. I believe this became one of my father's significant driving forces to succeed. He not only wanted to create a better life for his kids but wanted to allow them to enjoy sports and extracurricular activities at school and church.

My mother had also been born into a loving Christian

family. She was a woman who loved and lived life to its fullest. She enjoyed a great practical joke, loved to laugh, and loved to invest in people's lives. She always had an encouraging word for her children and for women who sought out her counsel.

Anneta Allen wrote this about my mother:

I loved your mom so much. Never had a friend like her in all these years. Anytime you were with her you knew

1. you were going to have fun,
2. you knew were going to laugh,
3. you knew you were going to spend money, and
4. you knew you might, just might, get into trouble.

Connie Rensberger wrote this about my mother:

Connie was one of the most generous and selfless people I've ever known. She was also the most encouraging and supportive person in my life during a very horrible time. She offered me strength, support, and rock-solid friendship while I was in an abusive marriage, which ultimately ended in divorce; and there was no judgment from her, ever.

I had never considered going to college, but she encouraged me to enroll, and she said, "If you'll go, I'll go!" And we went! Because of that one huge decision, my life was totally changed. I've had opportunities that would have never occurred, otherwise. (Oh, and I was a first-generation college graduate, thanks to Connie!) I even met my future husband, Bruce, in one of my college classes!... Then Connie was our wedding coordinator before "wedding coordinator" was even a thing! She was simply the best.

Around 1958 my father met my mother, Connie, at church camp. Mom wasn't shy about sharing with us how she didn't care for Dad at first. The hardworking farm boy was away from the daily oversight of his dad and his daily chores, and I'm guessing it was only natural that mischief followed him.

Loren Unruh and Connie Yeubanks married in January of 1963. They worked hard and provided a great home environment for their three children: me, Shawnda (two years later), and Krista (three years after Shawnda).

My father's Christian upbringing was put to the test. Early and rapid success led him into a time of more self-reliance, and over time he came to think he could make it on his own. But one dreadful trip from Montana would forever change his life, providing a lesson he never forgot.

My father inherited an entrepreneurial spirit, and at the age of twenty, he bought one combine and one truck. He put everything on the line and traveled four hundred miles across the Texas state line to start a custom combining business for the annual wheat harvest.

He had no customers—not even a potential customer. He just knew how to work hard, driven by a dream, so he started knocking on farmers' doors in search of wheat that needed to be cut.

Even as he chased his career dream, my father was also pursuing the beautiful woman who had swept him off his feet and had recently moved to Great Bend. Their start might have been rocky and their connection unlikely with that first awkward encounter at church camp, but over time a spark ignited into a flame that led to a powerful marriage ordained by God, where each one complemented the other. Together, they made a fantastic team, pursuing their dreams and God.

Working as a custom harvester means a nomadic lifestyle. Wheat harvest started in Texas in late May, and my parents followed the wheat crops as they ripened, working their way all the way up to Montana by early September. They returned home after the long summer to convert the combines, so they could move on to the next crop of corn, beans, or milo for the fall.

The first summer of their marriage, my mother had stayed back in Great Bend to work her job, which provided a steady and consistent income. By the time my dad got to town in late June, she had had enough of him being away and quit her job to join him in the nomadic harvest life.

She traveled with him every summer after that until I started school and carried a tireless load. She fixed breakfast for the men in their trailer every morning, then prepared lunch and supper, and delivered it to the crew in the field. Seven days a week, all summer long. There were no days off; even on rainy days, the men still had to eat.

Combines not cutting wheat meant lost income. It was essential to keep machines moving, so the majority of days the truck drivers ate first, and then they jumped on a combine to keep it cutting wheat while the combine drivers stopped to grab a hot meal out of the trunk of the car.

Weather permitting, the crew was up at 7 a.m. for breakfast, then to the field to do basic maintenance and start cutting wheat; and they didn't quit until ten o'clock or later. On a few occasions, I recall cutting until after 2 a.m., usually because we were pushing to beat an oncoming storm. The days were long, travel was constant, and the machines took daily abuse from all the hours they were cutting.

God had bigger plans for my dad, but it took a costly and miserable trip home from his last stop in Montana in the fall of 1965 to get his attention. Since starting out on his own, my father had found great success. He was hardworking and very determined to make it. But with those early successes, it was easy to slowly let self-reliance sneak in.

My dad will say that he was under heavy conviction

during this harvest season, because he had been drifting from his Christian walk. My mother was lovingly support-ing and encouraging him and praying for him. His older brother, who was a minister, was in between churches and came to Montana to help him finish the harvest. This only added to his conviction that he needed to get things right with God. But, like many of us at times in our lives, he was still holding out.

Toward the end of wheat harvest, an employee rolled a truck in the ditch, bending its frame. (Thank the Lord, the employee was not hurt.) Fortunately, they could still drive it carefully on the highway, though it was a challenge.

Finishing the harvest in Montana, the crew loaded up everything and begin the long trip home. He left Montana on what was, typically, a three-day trip. But this time, travel took five grueling days. Each day it became clearer some-thing was wrong with the engine on that truck that was rolled; as it got closer to home, it could barely climb the small hills of Kansas.

At this time, he owned two trucks, and each truck had a combine loaded in its bed. Each truck was also pulling a header trailer behind it. He had a vehicle towing the trailer house and another vehicle following. With just those vehi-cles and trailers, he experienced an unbelievable fifteen flat tires coming home.

Then, a header trailer came loose from the truck and obliterated an old wooden trailer on the other side of the road. Fortunately, it did not hit the truck pulling it, and there were no injuries.

Dad and his crew came limping back home, licking their wounds. Not only did the trip cost him time and extra money on repairs, but his machinery was now in such bad condition that he lost a very profitable job cutting milo in western Kansas. It was one disaster after another, and things were looking bleak for a young entrepreneur who had started out with such high hopes and early success.

On top of all of that, my parents were due to have their first child in March. Dad clearly understood he was in a tight spot with the recent setback and a child on the way.

God often uses our dark times to grab our attention. Dad now realized he could not run his business on his own; he needed God's favor and guidance.

While my parents were back in Great Bend, contemplating the next career move, my Dad surrendered his life to Christ and started attending church again faithfully—and has never looked back. The Lord miraculously opened up a new door for him and his dad to cut buffalo grass seed that winter in western Kansas.

This blessing became a juggling act, with my mother pregnant with me and my dad in western Kansas providing for his family and yet wanting to make sure he was home for the birth. The winter job proved to be very profitable, though, and allowed Dad to update his worn-out trucks and combines and optimistically prepare for the upcoming summer harvest season. What seemed possibly an end to his dreams turned out to be a moment when he fully understood the power of self-surrendering to God.

God continued to cast great favor on him, and by the time he was twenty-four, he owned five combines and five trucks. God had blessed him abundantly for his faithfulness and steadfastness, and he always gave generously from God's blessings.

The family was growing and school was getting ready to start for me; as a result, traveling became much more burdensome. Dad took on a partner for his harvesting crew, and my parents had a wild idea to start a restaurant. Neither one of them had any clue about the restaurant business or how to effectively run one.

But God was faithful and put several divine appointments in their path at just the right time to teach them and help them launch their restaurant business. They spent six weeks away from us, being trained by two different facilities while we stayed with our pastors at the time, Rev. Dean and Edith McCormick.

The restaurant opened in 1970; it was called the Black Angus Steak Ranch. My dad grew up only knowing how to work hard, and he possessed a drive to provide a better life for his family. This required much sacrifice. Before he could afford to hire a manager, he was it. He dropped us off at school and then headed to work, and most days he stayed there until closing time at 11 p.m.

Many of the early days in the restaurant business, the only time we were able to see my father was if we dropped by work. He always managed to stop whatever he was doing and take time to sit down with us. That always made me feel special. Before long, he hired a manager, and that allowed him more flexibility to be at home.

In 1972, a drive-in restaurant that sat adjacent to his restaurant came up for sale—The Big Wheel. He bought the business and dove into it with his normal big vision for his new project. Business was strong, so he decided to add on a small dining room.

Things were about to abruptly change. Shortly after he added the addition, a then little-known franchise began popping up throughout the Midwest. When McDonald's opened up in our small town, the Big Wheel took an instant hit to their business, losing half of their volume almost overnight. On top of that, Dad's trusted manager was diagnosed with a brain tumor and died within a few months. Dad simply couldn't keep the restaurant open. He walked over one day and locked the doors. This dream was over, and all he had accomplished was to add more debt to pay off.

It was quite a setback for a young man who had experienced great success thus far in his young business career. But when you are faithful and generous, God always has a plan, and this closing actually became a monstrous blessing in disguise.

My dad had become very involved in the church and always believed in being a faithful giver, which I know opened the doors of heaven to bless him even more. He had proven he could handle finances, and he always found ways to be extra generous with his giving.

He was serving on the church board and on the church building committee, which led him to meet Ed Pyle, of Pyle Construction Company. This was a divine appointment. My dad had been exploring the idea of opening a pizza restaurant on the lifeless Big Wheel site. Ed told him one day that what he really needed to do was build a motel on that spot.

This was a game changer for my mom and dad.

On the very same lot where their dream appeared to have taken a big hit, they erected a forty-eight-unit motel. Isn't that just like what God does? When we see the end of a dream, God uses that very thing to build a new dream in our life, to give us new purpose and meaning.

In 1977, they opened the Best Western Angus Inn, adjacent to the Black Angus Steak Ranch. Dad began with forty-eight rooms, and by 1980 he had expanded to ninety rooms, added an indoor pool, and expanded his banquet room at the restaurant to be able to serve about three hundred.

He became a successful businessman while running the family farm and a custom combining crew; at his peak, he had two restaurants and three motels.

This poor farm boy with just a high school diploma, who struggled at times with basic school studies, became an unlikely addition to the Best Western International board of directors for six years and chairman of the board for one year. As chairman, he stood before thousands of Best Western owners and managers and delivered an inspiring speech on the status and direction of the company. This position also allowed him to travel the world and meet many great people, businessmen, celebrities, and even the former president George W. Bush, who was the keynote speaker the year Dad was chairman of the board.

Tragedy strikes, life happens, financial crisis creates hardships. How do we respond? Many times, these events are lessons that help shift our lives back in a direction toward God.

God is able to build dreams, even on vacant, useless lots that appear to have lost their purpose.

CHAPTER 3

Transformation

RARELY DO YOU FIND a football offensive/defensive lineman who transitions to starting point guard for the basketball team. Lineman are big and strong. Point guards are smaller and fast.

All my life I had played on the offensive and defensive lines. I wasn't fast enough to be a linebacker and weighed too much to play any other skilled position.

My sophomore year of high school, I lettered in football for my role as a backup defensive tackle on varsity and also played nearly every down as the starting center, that same year, on the offensive line for our junior varsity team. More than likely, I was in line to be the next starting center on varsity.

When it came time for basketball my sophomore year, I was on the C team. Not tall enough to play down low, and too big and slow to be a true guard on the junior varsity.

But the summer before my junior year, I hit a growth spurt and started losing weight. I began working out and playing basketball nearly every day. By the time my junior year rolled around, I had made what was a shocking decision to many. I decided to give up football and focus on basketball. Even my dad was caught off guard by my decision.

My high school basketball coach told me years later how crazy he thought I was to give up a chance to be good at football, only to sell out for basketball and most likely never see any varsity playing time. My coach admits he basically gave me zero chance to succeed at basketball. Even though I had trimmed up, he still saw the slow defensive lineman.

But by the time basketball season rolled around, I was listed as the starting point guard on the JV team, and by the end of the year I was getting some limited minutes on the varsity squad.

If that transformation seems almost impossible, my spiritual transformation was even more improbable. Being raised in a Christian home was a great experience—one I am very grateful for. But as a teen, I struggled with trying to live out my faith while also trying to fit in. Every Christian battles this at some level, whether at work or school, with friends or family. I had some close friends at church, but when it came to school, I always felt like I was just on the outside of the circle, looking in. So close yet so far.

The easy way out for me was always to blame my parents: "I can't go to that party because my parents won't let me." It wasn't until later, when God radically changed my life, that I found myself no longer blaming my parents for things I couldn't do; instead, these rules became personal convictions.

If the church doors were open, I was there. Even though church wasn't always high on my personal agenda as a kid, this was not an option. Often, I might be right in the middle of a thrilling game of football in our front yard, on the final drive for the "championship," but had to drop everything to go to church. Many days looked similar: school, sports practice, supper, church, homework, bed.

Toward the end of my freshman year, the drift toward the crowd escalated. I desperately wanted to fit in and was tired of always feeling like I was on the outside. I became more like a double agent living a double life. I learned to act one way at church and a completely different way at school, trying to fit in both places and yet having no clue who I really was.

By the beginning of my junior year of high school, fitting in became my top priority. The path to destruction is never overnight; it is a gradual decline. Many times, we have no idea how far we have slid down until we can't see up anymore. Little did I know how deeply I would sink.

By that spring, I was in all-out rebellion. I went from one grounding to another; it was a never-ending cycle. I finally reached the point where I didn't even care about being grounded anymore. After all, I was seventeen, and I knew just about everything there was to know in life.

My mother, who was an incredible godly woman, sensed I was at a pivotal point in my life and very close to turning away from my faith and living life the way I wanted to. Everything my parents had tried to do that could help me had failed desperately.

The two worlds finally collided in early May when I had just finished my high school variety show. I decided I was going to go out with my friends and celebrate, whether my parents said yes or no. I called my dad to inform him of my decision, and he told me it was a bad choice, and if I did it anyway, I needed to return my car.

I walked to the back door of the restaurant. As he came out to meet me, I tossed my keys at him, ran to a friend's car waiting close by, and took off. To this day, I still can see my dad running down the street, chasing after the car. Nevertheless, I attended our variety show party and finally headed home around 2 a.m.

What I fully expected when I got home was a full-out war—and I was geared up and fully prepared for the battle. I had had enough, and I was ready to fight for my independence.

What I found when I walked in the back door completely caught me off guard and disarmed my building rage. My mother had been praying; she had decided to combat this night's rebellion with love. I walked into the house, and there she was, standing at the kitchen sink as I walked by with a stone-cold face. She didn't have to say any actual words; her eyes said it all. I'll never forget those eyes piercing straight through me that night. They showed the deep hurt she had for her son—a son she loved so much, who was heading down a path of destruction and breaking my parents' hearts.

I continued on past her, expecting a confrontation with my dad on the way to my room, but he was still out looking for me. I opened the door to my room and was shocked by what I saw. Everything was picked up, bed was made, and my mother had pulled the covers back on the side where I slept, so I could just crawl right in.

I was prepared for the fight but not prepared for the depths of love and forgiveness I experienced that night. It started to break something in me. The battle wasn't over, but the look in my mom's eyes was chipping away at a hardened heart.

The next day, I was once again grounded, but my parents were strategically walking a little softer. They felt if they could just get me to youth camp, God would get through to me. As it turned out, the breakthrough didn't happen that particular week, but God put things into motion.

So often, when we pray for things, we see the answer happening a certain way. When it doesn't happen on our timeline or the manner we suspected, it can easily be discouraging. God answers prayers but—in my experience—rarely as we had envisioned the answer.

My parents must have felt some of that discouragement as I came home from camp unchanged. So much prayer and hope had been put into me going, and nothing, as far as they could see, had changed.

What did happen was that shortly after arriving at camp, I was walking down the sidewalk and passed an incredible-looking blonde. I did an about-face. I had to meet her!

We introduced ourselves; her name was Tamela. We quickly connected at a deep level, and there was little doubt that love was in the air. I was a pro at playing the "I'm a great Christian" game. I had spent years perfecting the art. As far as she knew, she had just found a great Christian young man.

That week at camp, I went to the altar after each sermon, like a good Christian kid. My heart was softening, but my sinful nature was still unwilling to surrender control.

Tamela was from the Wichita area. I knew my parents would not say no to me if I wanted to go back to Wheat State Camp to see some friends at week number two. Wheat State Camp was just a way to manipulate them; in reality, I primarily wanted to see Tamela again.

I could not tell you who the preacher was that night or even a word he said during his sermon. I sat in the last row, and because I was technically a guest, I didn't think I had to play the game that night and had no intentions whatsoever of responding to the altar call.

But the Holy Spirit had something else in mind; he directed the speaker to call everyone down to the altar. This threw my game plan off a little, and my mind was spinning with how to respond. At first, I thought, *Whatever. He just means every camper who's there for the week.*

Then I thought, *Oh well, I can play this game one more time,* and started to make the familiar insincere walk to the altar. About halfway down, the Spirit of God overcame me, and I literally took off running to the altar and began to cry out to God. I spent well over an hour at the altar that night. It was the wildest thing I had ever experienced, and to this day, it still seems like a blur. I dropped Tamela off at her house and made the two-hour drive back home. I arrived around 2 a.m., overflowing with God's unconditional love and forgiveness because I had finally "self-surrendered" to His call.

My heart had become so hardened and full of rebellion, but the firm love from my dad and the gentler love from my mother sparked a change in me and started a process of softening my heart. In the answer to their many prayers, God put an incredible woman in my life to finish the process and placed me where the power of God's Spirit overcame me.

A radical transformation took place that night. I entered a sinner with a hardened heart, and I left a new man with a new heart.

How does someone go from being a defensive tackle/center on the football team to a starting basketball point guard? How does God take a hardened sinner and transform his life and purpose?

Defensive tackle to point guard really is an excellent picture of what Christ does for us when we sell out and fully commit. We are all sinners and have struggled at times to find God's plan for our lives. But when we finally let God get ahold of our lives and transform us, He gives our lives meaning and purpose, which allows us to go on to do great things for Him. We can defy all the odds, and through Christ, become someone people could not have recognized a few years ago. We are transformed into His image! What an awesome thing!

I entered my senior year of high school on fire and sold out for Christ. For the first time in a long time, I no longer cared what everyone thought of me. I was going to live for Christ.

CHAPTER 4

Blindsided

I SPENT SO MUCH TIME STRIVING to fit in with the crowd, but when I got there, I realized I was just another person in the crowd following along and acting like every other kid was. When I surrendered my life entirely to Christ, I no longer was seeking the recognition of others or awards. I was striving to please Christ, and in my desire to follow and please Him, Christ exalted me.

I decided to follow Christ no matter the cost; my former goals were no longer my goals. I was going to live for Him, even if I was the only person doing so. When I laid down my desires and put His desires above mine, then God began to grant me favor.

I give Christ all the glory for the doors that opened. When I tried to do it on my own, I failed miserably. This was Christ in me, the hope of glory (Colossians 1:27)!

I never want to come across as bragging about myself or accomplishments. After all, I tried it on my own. The accomplishments are simply bragging about what God can do with a changed life!

One example of this is that I was nominated for homecoming king my senior year. I had never been remotely in that conversation before. Looking back, I realize that friends saw something different in me—they saw the transformation Christ had performed. I wasn't just another person seeking to fit in and gain glory for myself anymore. My pursuit was toward more of Jesus, and I wasn't concerned about what everyone thought of me. Through my pursuit of Christ, He honored me, but the rewards weren't nearly as important to me as they were before.

The varsity basketball team was deep with seven seniors. I had always been on the tail end of that group, and four of those seniors started or had significant playing time the year before at the varsity level; the other two were ahead of me on the JV rotation. There was one starting position open: point guard.

When we sell out to God, He blesses us with the desires of our heart. I was named the starting point guard on a team that went 17–5 that year, ranked in the top five in class 6A for a good part of that year, and was named second team all-conference. I eventually went on to play college basketball, something I simply loved doing. But all the glory goes to God; when He transforms us, it opens up a whole new world of His favor on our lives!

I was on life's mountaintop, experiencing God's favor, enjoying life, only to be punched in the gut. In the midst of this incredible season of life, I was hit with news no one wants to hear.

It was late January on a Wednesday morning, before school, my mother came into my room and told me she was not going to be at my game on Friday. This was entirely out of character for her; my parents rarely missed any game or event that any of their kids were participating in.

We suffered our first loss of the season to McPherson that Friday night, but I was about to be blindsided with something worse. As I approached the locker room door, there stood my dad. This definitely wasn't normal, and before he could say a word, my gut began to ache. Something was really wrong. He pulled me to the side and told me my mother had breast cancer; she'd had a lump removed in surgery earlier that day. The shock left me speechless. My mind was trying to grasp what I just heard. The "cancer" word is such a scary one.

It was a long and silent ride back to Great Bend on the team bus. My teammates offered their support. But my faith and fear were already clashing. *Why now, God? Why during such a fantastic year? Why?*

My mother was a strong woman of faith, always concerned more about everyone else than herself. She didn't want me to miss out on playing basketball that night or interrupt what was a great senior year. When she reflected on her own battle with the news, her main focus was her concern for everyone else. She wrote in a journal during this time:

> Finding the lump, my mind just sorta blanked. You want to think that this is just a dream. This kind of thing just can't happen. I have three beautiful kids that need me. How would they make it without me? Loren is so busy, he will not be able to give them the time they need. And Loren, who will take care of him? We are so close; how will he handle this? Lord, they need me. You can't do this. And then it dawns on me: "You don't get to call the shots. God is omnipotent, and He doesn't make mistakes."
>
> Who is going to finish their scrapbooks? The stuff isn't even sorted. And their rooms aren't finished the way they want them. Loren will never have time to do these things. Then Loren, how do I tell him? We have stockholders meeting at the restaurant on Tuesday and the church business meeting Wednesday night and then Rick has games Thursday, Friday, and Saturday, and then we leave for Phoenix on Sunday.
>
> Why now, Lord? This really isn't real, is it? But it is. I won't worry Loren tonight. I'll go to the doctor tomorrow and see what he says. Maybe it's nothing,

and I won't have to tell him. I just want to go to sleep,
so I don't have to think.

The up-and-down journey of cancer is wearying. But we
were a family of faith, so after the initial shock wore off,
there wasn't a huge burden on me because I felt completely
confident that God was going to take care of Mom. This
was going to be a great testimony of how God heals.

I finished my senior year on fire for God, looking forward to a new chapter in college and doing great things for
God while pursuing my calling.

That summer, I went back for my last year at Wheat State
Camp. I again experienced a new encounter with God and
knew I had a call into the ministry.

Through all this, I was still dating the woman God had
used to help change the course of my life. I received yet
another honor from the transformation God had started
in me. Tamela and I were crowned church camp king and
queen that year. The future looked bright.

That very same summer, God placed someone else in
my path with whom I quickly developed a strong friendship—a man who still plays an important role in my life
thirty years later. He threw me a lifeline when I didn't even
realize I needed one. Billy Thomas, a young, on-fire youth
pastor/evangelist, "just happened" to be my counselor that
year. (I don't believe in "just happens"; God set up a divine
appointment that sparked a lifelong friendship.)

That fall, I left for Bible college with big dreams of how
God was going to use me. Ready to conquer the world! My
senior year was just a launching point for what God had
planned for me!

CHAPTER 5

Cracker Jack Prize?

IN THE FALL OF 1984, I began classes at Central Bible College, full of big dreams and the youthful desire to save the world!

My relationship with Tamela took a new twist. We weren't just two hours apart; we were now five hours away from each other. I carried a heavy schedule with school and basketball team practices and a thirty-seven-game schedule. She had an equally challenging schedule, with high school, cheerleading duties, and working a part-time job.

It was 1984, so there was no internet or texting available. We had to sit down and handwrite letters or talk on the phone, which we did as often as we could, but long-distance phone calls were expensive at that time. Young people today will never know the pain of having one pay phone on the entire dorm floor and hoping someone was around to answer it if your girlfriend called. Our hi-tech intercom system involved yelling down the hall to see if the person being called was in. If you were lucky, the guy who answered the phone took time to leave a note if you'd missed a call.

Little did I know that God was using this time with my future wife to create a strong foundation, built on a deep friendship, stemming from all our communications through letters. The foundation was being laid for when our love was tested to the very core many years later.

My freshman year was a great year in so many ways. It

felt good to be in a Bible college, preparing for the dreams God had placed in my heart. I was classmates with some world changers and getting to play basketball, the game I loved.

Our basketball team ended up falling short and finishing second in the nation, losing to Cincinnati Bible in the championship.

Even though we lost, it capped off an amazing year. I was loving every moment of college and the lifelong friends I was making. I was preparing to be a world changer too!

I returned home for the summer, working on the farm and with my dad's custom harvesting crew. I was in love, and I had a ring that I needed to get purchased so I could ask Tamela to be my wife! I was highly motivated to put in as many hours as I possibly could.

I also started traveling to preach whenever invited. I especially thrived on speaking to youth groups and grabbed every opportunity I could. I also participated in some short-term missions trips to reach the lost.

On one of those trips, I'll never forget the guilt I felt. Our ministry team had traveled all the way to St. Louis to street-witness in the inner-city areas. It was a really hot day, and we had yet to spark a meaningful conversation with anyone about Christ. We stumbled across some young men playing a pickup game of basketball in the park. Several of the guys playing had to leave, and by divine appointment, they asked some of us to play.

I love a good game of basketball, but I was thinking, *God, we drove all this way to minister to people, and here I am playing a game of basketball. What a waste!* We played for well over an hour, and during that course of time, we started building comradery and respect with the young men. When the game was over, we were able stay another hour and witness to each of them about the love of Christ.

It's so easy to put ministry in a box; I wonder how many

times we miss opportunities. What if we had just kept walking and said, "Thanks, but we are here to witness for Christ and we don't have time for games"? I learned from this experience to be sensitive to God opening doors for divine appointments to share the good news.

I entered my sophomore year of college in the fall of 1985 with high expectations for what God was going to continue to do in my life. I was elected class vice president. We were returning most of our players on the basketball team and adding some as well; we had high hopes of chasing a national title. But the best highlight of the year was that Tamela and I were finally in the same town, attending the same college for the first time in our two-year relationship. She tried out for and made the basketball cheerleading squad, which meant we could spend more time together on the road trips to and from the out-of-town games.

Life was great, the love of my life was on the same campus, the outlook for our basketball team was promising, my mother's cancer was retreating, and our faith was strong. It was a great season in our lives.

Although I planned to wait awhile to ask Tamela the big question, I've never been very good at keeping gifts for long, so I didn't waste much time. Shortly after the fall semester started, I popped the big question.

I took Tamela out to the most romantic restaurant in Springfield, Missouri: "Mexican Villa"! Okay, it wasn't the most romantic, but it was *our* favorite restaurant and popular among the college students, thanks to good, inexpensive Mexican food.

Before we left for supper that night, I took a gummy worm (one of our favorite snacks) out of the bag, taped a note on it (written on a foil gum wrapper)—"Will you marry me?"—and then attached the engagement ring to the worm.

My seemingly flawless plan almost didn't happen because we overate that night—way too many chips. The last thing either one of us wanted was a gummy worm after that. Maybe this wasn't the best plan, and I needed to rethink it and save the proposal for another day.

As we were driving closer to campus, I started forcing a few worms down and finally convinced her to eat one. *Thank You, Lord*, because I sure couldn't force many more down! She reached into the bag and grabbed "the one." It was dark in the car. As she grabbed the worm, I remember her saying, "Hey, there's a prize attached to this worm; this is just like a box of Cracker Jacks!" Turning on the light for her, I told her she probably needed to look a little closer. She read the note and saw the ring, and the rest is history. She got her prize, and we were married in August of 1986.

In January of 1986, just over midway through my sophomore basketball season, I severely rolled my ankle. X-rays showed that I had broken my ankle, and the injury sidelined me until just before the playoffs. It was devastating news.

Amid bad news, there was also a blessing. My mother's cancer had returned, and she had not been doing very well. The blessing was that since I didn't have the obligations of basketball, it allowed me to spend more time at home with my mom on weekends and breaks.

The only constant on the merry-go-round of cancer is that there is no constant. Though we feared we might be getting closer to the end if there weren't a miracle, once again my mother's health started improving, and around the same time, my ankle healed just in time for the playoffs.

We had big hopes, but our team took a devastating blow when one of our starting big men tore his ACL, putting him, now, out of commission for the playoffs. We fell short once again, finishing second in the nation to the same team for the second straight year, Cincinnati Bible.

School was out, and plans for the wedding were in full swing. Although Tamela and I had contemplated waiting another year or so to get married, we decided because of my mother's health that we should get married that year.

I returned home to work on the farm and for my dad's harvest crew again before the big day in August. Most summers fly by, but this summer seemed like it was moving at a snail's pace. After finally getting to spend so much time together in college, Tamela and I were not able to see each other very much that summer, since we were both busy working to pay for the wedding and honeymoon and living two hours apart.

My mother was feeling better and super excited about the wedding. In hindsight, I wonder if maybe she was just grateful someone was actually taking me!

There was great anticipation for the rehearsal dinner and wedding from people looking forward to paybacks. My dad and my mother loved a good practical joke, and they were both involved in playing many pranks on brides and grooms before or even on their wedding days. Attendance at my wedding was not going to be a problem because they were plenty of people anxious to repay the "favor."

Susan Dunlap, who was from Kentucky and had met Kevin (her future husband) from Great Bend at Bible college writes:

> You know the Great Bend tradition of kidnapping the bride at the wedding and driving them around for an hour. These pranks did not happen at my church, and my parents were not fans of this, so they stuck close by my side that day. The men, including your dad, had already kidnapped Kevin, so we thought I was safe. As my parents walked me outside, your mother and Cindy—whom I had recently met and were two people who I *thought* I could trust—came up by my side, ever so trusting, reassuring me everything was fine, only to my dismay to be tricked and escorted to the kidnapping-car-in-waiting, which then drove me around for an

hour, away from my new husband. Connie always kept life interesting.

Bruce and Connie Rensbergers wrote this:

We had noticed our car was completely covered in "Joy" dishwashing liquid after the wedding, so when we got to Hutchinson to spend the night at the Holidome, we stopped by a full-service car wash to have them rinse all the soap off. They had to spray that car I-don't-even-know-how-many times, because every time they started to hand-dry it (it was before wind turbines were invented), it would just lather up again. I think they eventually gave up on getting it rinsed completely. The next morning, we woke up to near-zero temps. When we were ready to leave, we found our car doors were completely frozen shut. The wind was blowing what seemed to be a hundred miles an hour, I swear; and the matches we were trying to use to thaw the locks kept going out. We finally asked maids for extension cords to reach from the nearest outlet inside the hotel to connect my hair dryer to thaw those locks. I can still hear Connie "cackling" about that to this day. She was one mess, and I loved her so much. She could have written, produced, directed, and starred in *Pranked*. She always made life so much fun.

After we finished the rehearsal dinner, those seeking revenge for pranks my parents had played on their wedding, wasted no time before they took me away for the evening, they were going to throw me in the hotel pool. Of course, they were kind enough to let me take out my wallet and remove my shoes before getting wet. I tried to fight the idea of going into the pool initially but realized it was clearly a losing battle. So I quit fighting, grabbed the man closest to me, Mark Davis, and gave him a big ol' bear hug as ten or so other men pushed us both into the pool. The poor guy didn't have the luxury of pulling his wallet out or taking off his watch and shoes.

My dad and several others were the kings of bachelor night pranks. There was the time they dropped a guy in the country; when they finally headed back to get him (about ten minutes later), he wasn't having any of it and hid from them, opting to walk back to town, ending the party early. Or there was the guy who had a nice new car and refused to bring it to the wedding because he didn't want it decorated. When several men found out he was staying only about an hour away, they made sure his car was decorated when he woke up the next morning. It was fun—a harmless game of cat and mouse.

My pranksters drove me all over town with lots of threats of what they were going to do to me for paybacks. The men told my dad later that it really wasn't that much fun driving me around, because I wasn't fighting anything they were going to do and was fully cooperating with their plans. I knew there was no way I could win the fight with them, so I just played along.

After a storybook wedding in which I married the woman of my dreams, we headed to Acapulco for our honeymoon and then straight back to CBC to pursue God's call on our lives. My father and mother were so supportive and excited for us both. My wife was working at Dillard's, and I was attending classes in the morning and working in the afternoons at the school carpentry shop. Life was going just like we planned.

My mother-in-law came down for a visit later that fall of 1986. While my wife was preparing a Bundt cake for breakfast, she became very nauseous and had to lie down. And then I heard my mother-in-law utter these words to my wife: "Are you pregnant?" The look of shock on Tamela's face left me wondering if life was about to radically change for us once again.

Everyone went home, and life went back to normal—except that my wife's nausea continued. She was throwing up so frequently, it was beginning affect her at work.

We scheduled a doctor's appointment to get an official opinion on what we had already presumed: Tamela was pregnant with our first child! We were so excited, but pregnancy was not kind to my wife, and the constant vomiting throughout her pregnancy, day and night, became her new norm. She battled major swelling late in her pregnancy that developed into preeclampsia/toxemia and caused complications in the delivery of our son.

My mother's health was doing well during the time leading up to our wedding, but once again, the merry-go-round of cancer was rolling, and although she hadn't told us yet, she was feeling poorly again.

In early October, we decided to tell my parents about the impending birth of their first grandchild, and my wife came up with a clever way to divulge the good news.

McDonald's used to have pumpkin Happy Meal buckets in October, so we purchased a package of newborn diapers and placed one inside the bucket, attaching a card that read, "Is this a trick or a treat?" The news of Mom's first grandchild made her grin from ear to ear; she was ecstatic. She wasted no time in starting to purchase gifts, including a wooden rocking horse and silver teddy bear bank, and she even began knitting an afghan for her first grandchild.

I was so happy: we were married with our first child on the way, we were pursuing God's call on my life, and my mother's health and spirits were once again strong.

But by the time we came home for Thanksgiving, it was apparent things were in rapid decline, and the news that the cancer was back with a vengeance and spreading rapidly was devastating. It felt like a thankless Thanksgiving, but that wouldn't be our last brutal Thanksgiving.

By the time we returned for Christmas break, Mom was being put back into the hospital. Hospice was not available like it is today.

The alarm bell rang loudly, prayer warriors arose from all over the area, and they went to battle in prayer. They rallied and raised their banners and flooded heaven with prayers for my faithful mother. Mom had never strayed from God in her life, and even now, in the battle for her life, she refused to talk about anything except that God was going to raise her out of that bed and heal her. Later, my dad admitted there were things he wished they would have talked about, in case Mom wasn't healed, but she did not allow it. God was going to allow her to walk out of that hospital, end of discussion.

CHAPTER 6

The Unmerry Christmas

I WAS BACK AT SCHOOL, and it felt like with each passing day we received additional bad reports of how Mom's cancer was spreading. Despite the adverse news, she continued to believe for her healing, and the prayer warriors continued to cover her in prayers.

She was in the hospital the entire time we were home for semester break, except for the few hours she was released to come home for Christmas Day. She had always made the holidays so special for us. She loved Christmas, and to say she went overboard each year is an understatement.

It was a difficult day for Mom. She wasn't feeling well, and I know it pained her that on one of her favorite holidays she couldn't provide us with the typical activities we were accustomed to. Because of this stress, her usual positive attitude, and joyous smile were missing in action that day. This was one of the few times she allowed us to see that side of her. In spite of her faith and strength, it was an Unmerry Christmas for her.

For us kids, it was still a special day. We got to spend Christmas with Mom at home rather than in the hospital. We didn't care about the gifts; our greatest gift was being with her and celebrating our Savior's birth as a family.

During the rest of break, we spent as much time as possible with her at the hospital. As the time was getting closer to go back, there wasn't a bone in my body that wanted to leave my mother's side. I'll never forget what she said to me: "I went to Bible college for a year, and because of finances, I was never able to go back. It has been my dream and my prayer that one of my kids finish Bible college. You are going back to school."

Torn between not wanting to leave her and not wanting to disappoint her, my wife and I reluctantly headed back to school. I knew there were great people covering her in prayer, and it was in God's hands. God was going to heal her.

Early in the new year, Anneta Allan, a great friend, drove up from their new home in Texas to spend the day with mom. Although she was there to cheer up my mother, she ended up encouraged by my mother's faith and laughter. She writes:

> The one day that I treasure to this day was in January, 1987. We came to Great Bend knowing it would be our last time to see and talk to her this side of heaven. Loren made it possible for Connie and I to have the whole day in her hospital room by ourselves. He took Jimmy to "wrangle" cows for the day and left us girls to talk. Connie had told me the night before, when we first got there, that she hated when people came to see her with their hair fixed all pretty and all dressed up. So, the next morning I came into her room with the largest and ugliest flannel gown I had found in a store there. I found leopard-like large house shoes and I rolled my hair in pink sponge rollers. When I walked into her room, I crawled into bed with her, laid my head on her shoulder, and told her I just hated to dress up to go visit people in the hospital and I knew she wouldn't mind if I came as I was. Of course, she loved that, and we laughed and laughed about that. I will never forget that day. We talked about the fun times we had shared and, yes, the trouble we had got into together. We talked about how good the Lord was and how HE had carried her, and

she shared Scriptures that had carried her in the night hours when her faith was tested. I started to cry, and she would say, "Look here, we are not having any of that! STOP THAT!" You feel you are there to encourage her, but often she was the one encouraging others. That room was filled with the presence of Almighty God. I just know that God was smiling down on us the day we became friends AND then HE told the angels "better keep an eye on those two." Because together we were surely trouble. Some thirty years later, I'm writing this with tears in my eyes because to think of Connie is to have a heart full of love and, yes, a heart that just has to smile.

A few weeks later I received the call I had long dreaded. My dad's office was in his restaurant, and he only closed the door for the toughest of conversations. I know this because he closed that door several times to talk with me when I was a rebellious teenager. I've often wondered what was racing through his mind that day. He was a strong man, a great leader. But he will tell you that most of his success wouldn't have happened without my mother by his side. They were an unstoppable team who complemented each other's strengths and weaknesses. Now, as the clock had nearly ticked its last stroke and the inevitable was at hand, he sat in the restaurant and office they had sacrificed so much to build together and dialed each of us to deliver the devastating news: the battle was over; it was time to come home. I'm sure at that moment it felt like the end of their dream. All the hours of labor and the hardships the two of them had survived, working together toward their common dreams, and now she was nearing her last breath.

My wife and I left Springfield, Missouri, with my sister Shawnda, who had transferred to CBC at the start of the semester. We clearly understood that, without a miracle, this was likely our last time to see Mom. After we arrived, we spent a few hours with her in the hospital, along with much of our extended family, but she was weary and heavily medicated to help control the severe pain she was in. The cancer had spread throughout her entire body. The joy she always expressed had finally faded, and this woman of God was not herself anymore. She was weary from the battle and the pain and fully prepared and at peace to meet her Savior.

Tamela and I decided to let her rest, so we went to my parents' house to catch a few hours of sleep. We planned to return in the morning, but after a while, we were awakened by footsteps in the hall. Deep down, I knew what it meant hearing that sound so early in the morning. My dad and our pastor J. P. McCamey delivered the crushing news. The battle was over; she was gone. This woman, so full of life and faith, always ready with the right words to encourage her family and friends—this woman who could light up a room—was gone way too early. And the questions inside begin to rise. *Why, God?*

It was a hard thing to see Dad—who had tirelessly been by her side while also trying to keep their businesses running, who had always been so strong—weeping, a man broken by the loss of the love of his life. So many memories they had had together, but now the reality setting in that there would be no new memories.

My mother passed away six days before my sister Krista's sixteenth birthday. Just like with Christmas, birthdays were another time she always went all out to make memories. On our sixteenth birthdays, she always did something extra special. Even on her deathbed, with massive painkillers in her body and not completely coherent at times, she was still planning one last birthday surprise—always thinking of her kids first.

Somehow, she managed to make sure birthday balloons were delivered to Krista at school, with a note attached to them. My sister experienced both great joy and great agony on that day as she was called to the office to pick them up—the joy of receiving her mom's deep love and one last memory to cherish, and yet the hurt that her mom wasn't there to celebrate this special day with her.

Krista describes her grief this way:

> My mom was an incredible woman. She was the type of woman that could be heard laughing from across the room, and you wondered what was so funny over there and wanted to be a part of it. She loved life and was involved in everything from playing the piano every Sunday at church (even when she had to bring her oxygen tank with her), to helping my dad run our restaurant and motel, to throwing parties at our house after football games so we would have somewhere safe and fun to hang out.
>
> I was twelve years old when I first found out my mom had cancer. I had stayed home sick from school the day that my mother went in for a biopsy, only to find out it was cancer. I remember my father calling my grandma to tell her they were going to be at the hospital a little longer, and I remember my grandma trying to explain why Mom was not coming home that day without truly explaining why. No one thought I would understand.
>
> At sixteen years old, I could not handle all the grief of the family. Everyone was sitting around my house and crying. I wanted life to be normal again. I NEEDED life to be normal again. I wanted to return to school and pretend that things were normal. I had to fight with my dad in order to return to school because he thought I should stay home, but I could not handle being in the house with everyone grieving all day. I understood what was going on. I knew I would not see my mother again,

but my thoughts were more about me and making my life seem normal—like any typical teenager.

As the months and years passed, yes, the grieving gets easier, but what I have found is that I miss her and grieve for her in new ways in every season of my life. When I graduated high school, I wished she were there. At my wedding, I wished she were there. When I had children of my own, I really wished she were there, and as my children grow, I miss her again and again and again. The grief never really goes away, but it does become easier to live with and talk about and help others along the way.

I tell my children stories about my mother all the time because I want them to know their grandmother, and through these stories, I find another little part of me heals. It would be so great if grieving were an "instant" process and we could just blink and feel better, but if you are reading this, then, most likely, you know firsthand how hard and long the process is. It has been twenty-two years since my mother passed away, and yes, there are days when it feels like I lost her yesterday, but slowly the good, happy memories outweigh the day of loss.

My other sister, Shawnda, wrote this about Mother:

Connie Lee Unruh. Dedicated, fighter, full of love, and continually pushed me and encouraged me.

There were so many more stories of things she simply did to embarrass me and my friends. Even in high school, we still got surprised by the things she pulled off and have no idea how she came up with all of them.

For some reason, Thanksgiving, Christmas, and birthdays were a priority, and she loved it all. I did pass this on to my kids. I decorated their rooms while they were asleep. My son slept right through it all, my daughter woke up sometimes and I was stuck on the floor in her room waiting for her to fall back asleep.

A few years ago, I started opening boxes that I had packed up for storage. The boxes have moved many times through many states. I had forgotten that Mom gave me a list of things to find of hers and hide them. I found these again, and a few years ago I read her journal again. She was so concerned about how Dad and us kids would be affected, about the dreams we had—and could we do it without her? While she was dying of cancer, her top concerns were only about her family.

Now, as for me, I was leaving for college at ORU in Tulsa, Oklahoma. When Dad and Mom drove me down in August 1986, she seemed to be doing so good. We had just finished my brother's wedding. She helped me decorate my dorm room and organize things. I never knew at that time that our daily "long-distance" phone calls and daily letters she wrote me were actually advice to guide me through the next chapter in my life.

I think the most humorous letter is the one that just said, "I got nothing to say today, but I wanted to imagine you running to your mailbox to read this insightful letter. Love, Mom." She always came up with such unique ways to bring a smile to us. Only Mom.

In all seriousness, she was preparing me for life as an adult and mother. Over the course of that semester, I could tell things were changing in our daily phone call, and she wasn't settled with something I said. A few days later, a letter came to explain further.

She was basically cramming everything she could into a three-month period. Dreams, aspirations, strength, goals, and building a family were the things she discussed with me. At the time, I was looking at music and a missions degree. It was interesting to learn that she also had wanted to go into missions, and it didn't happen for her, but she prayed that God would pass this passion on to one of her kids. It did not work out the way I had planned it, but I look at my brother, Rick, and I am amazed at what he has been through and now the ministry he is doing to help others, and I know Mom is smiling.

I only had eighteen years with her, which is far too short, but she crammed in so much of her love, support, and knowledge in that short time. She was so amazing.

Connie Rensberger wrote:

Two phone calls I'll never forget are ones that I received from Shawnda; the first one was telling me about Connie's diagnosis and surgery. The other phone call was the one I received at Calvary Assembly, Wichita, where I was music minister (and where I would NEVER have been had it not been for Connie's encouragement way back when). Shawnda called to tell me that Connie had passed away, and I heard the strength in her voice that she got from her mother. I have no words to describe my feelings when I heard that devastating news.

I still wonder why Connie was taken from us. This is a Scripture where I find comfort and want to share with you:

"But we do not want you to be uninformed, brothers, about those who are asleep, that you may not grieve as others do who have no hope. For since we believe that Jesus died and rose again, even so, through Jesus, God will bring with him those who have fallen asleep. For this we declare to you by a word from the Lord, that we who are alive, who are left until the coming of the Lord, will not precede those who have fallen asleep. For the Lord himself will descend from heaven with a cry of command, with the voice of an archangel, and with the sound of the trumpet of God. And the dead in Christ will rise first. Then we who are alive, who are left, will be caught up together with them in the clouds to meet the Lord in the air, and so we will always be with the Lord. Therefore encourage one another with these words." (1 Thessalonians 4:13–18)

When my mother died despite her unwavering faith of God's healing, my questions swirled in my head. Not only had she died that day, but part of my faith had died with her. *God, if You can't heal this incredible woman of God, who was full of faith and had so much life to share with others, then can You heal anyone?* The questions were more of a nagging whisper at first. But over the years, they took on more and more strength when I thought of her.

The seed of doubt had been planted, and my dreams of doing great things for God were slowly dying. And I never saw it happening.

CHAPTER 7

Life Goes On

ONE OF THE MOST ACCURATE STATEMENTS you will hear after losing a loved one is this: "Life goes on." Despite its accuracy, the statement feels harsh to those who are grieving, coming across as emotionless and uncaring (even though it's rarely intended that way). It doesn't feel like life goes on; in our hearts and minds at that moment, life as we've known it has come to a screeching halt.

Years after my mother's death, a couple was visiting our church. The pastor asked me to reach out to them, since we too had experienced a great loss. As I talked with them, they started to share how deeply wounded they were. They had attended a particular church for many years and felt they had some great friends within the church. Then their son committed suicide. Their pain was unimaginable, as were the unending regrets of "Why? What did we miss? Why didn't we see the signs?" Four months after his passing, they were pulled into a meeting with the elders and instructed that it was time to stop grieving because life goes on. They were crushed by some of their closest friends who couldn't find the compassion to try to understand why they were stuck, and instead of trying to walk them through their grieving, basically gave a cold-hearted command to move on.

When you're grieving, there are many days when you feel that time is frozen, and you are stuck in a pit of grief. Harsh hopelessness hangs over you. Life *will* go on, but it will never go on *as before.*

My wife and I didn't have much time to consciously grieve the loss of my mother. I was busy in school, preparing for the ministry. Tamela was pregnant with our first child, newly married, working a job, and dealing with all her health complications. In the midst of all this, I was trying to walk through my grief and a major attack on my faith. If we had not had a strong marital foundation built through three years of dating and God's unwavering love for us, I seriously doubt we could have made it through the many setbacks and sorrows we faced.

I mean it as a very high compliment when I say that my mother was going to be a "rotten grandmother"; she would have had all her grandkids spoiled rotten and helped them become masters at pranking their parents!

For someone who found so much joy in life, it's a shame that she never got to experience the unbelievable joy of holding her grandchildren. Even while she was sick, when she heard she was going to be a grandma, the economy in Great Bend saw a boost due to increased sales as she went out buying gifts for her first grandchild. The most precious gift she left was an afghan she was never able to complete herself. However, a close friend of hers took it and finished it in time for our son's birth.

My mother was completely convinced Tamela was the one for me. Mom did all she could to help keep me in line and to make sure I didn't mess up my relationship with my wife. She made sure I was sending flowers and getting her gifts and often sent me a check along with a note telling me to take her out for a nice dinner. Still, years after Mom's death, I now realize I could have handled things so much better in supporting my wife, but I was feeling lost myself. And, unfortunately, there are no rules to follow when grieving.

I finished my junior year of college, and the time came to

celebrate my firstborn son, Dake, who was born on June 1 (my wife's father's birthday), just a little over four months after my mother's death. The excitement was surreal: he was the perfect baby, a true gift from God.

In the midst of our great joy, my heart was saddened with the whispering in my head: *Grandma sure would have been proud of Dake!* Not only was my mother missing seeing her grandson, but I think it bothered me more that my son would never get to know what an amazing, fun-loving, crazy, God-loving grandmother he had. Dake would never fully understand the impact this great woman had on my life and on so many others who came in contact with her.

I spent that summer working on our family farm, preparing to go back to school for my senior year. The days were long, and many times Tamela brought Dake out to ride with me on the tractor or combine, or they would go visit my grandma at the farmhouse.

My grandfather had passed away when I was a freshman in high school, which was a devastating blow because we were so close, and I spent many hours out on the farm with them. My Uncle Vic stayed the first week with Grandma after my grandfather's passing, and then I spent close to a month with her after that so she did not have to be alone at night on the secluded farm.

In 1986, after only playing JV college basketball the previous year since I was newly married and focused on my mother's health, I decided I wanted to play varsity again for my senior year. I had fun, but I had definitely lost a step and couldn't play the game at the same level I was accustomed to.

About seven or eight games into the season, I was pulled into my coach's office; he was visibly upset. I was told I was not eligible and the team likely would have to forfeit all the games played so far in the season. The previous semester, I had only completed eleven credits, and I needed twelve. With the loss of my mother and so much missed school, I had stopped attending one of my music classes and never attempted to make it up; therefore, I was short on credits.

Sheer panic hit me. I had just caused my teammates a crushing blow to their season. My former roommate and teammate told me that when I came out of the coach's office, they knew something was wrong; my face was white as a ghost. I didn't say anything to anyone but left before practice started and headed to the academic dean.

While I was visiting with the dean and looking over my file, he found my written request for a credit for attending the Billy Graham School of Evangelism that summer in Denver. And he had approved it for one credit hour, which was exactly what I was short—but for some reason, it did not get transferred onto my transcript. I did actually have twelve credit hours. Crisis averted.

That fall, I had the honor to preach in senior chapel. I had dreamed about that day since I was a freshman, but in that dream, I had always envisioned my mother sitting in the audience with a big smile on her face, full of joy. Because her prayers had been answered, I finished Bible college. Yet there was the constant reminder in the back of my head, as I was preaching, of how proud my mother would have been to be at that service. Instead, I was left sharing a message on praise based upon her passing. I preached that our daily praise becomes a source of comfort, that praise keeps our eyes off the problem and focused on the great Comforter. I looked out from the pulpit that day and wanted so badly to see my mom's glowing face. She was always my number one supporter in entering the ministry. I pray God opened the curtain of heaven that day and let her get a glimpse of her answered prayers and her life still making an impact in others through mine.

I finished college in May, and my family headed to Indianapolis to complete my internship at Calvary Temple and to assist the Indiana state youth director, Dave Divine, at church camps. It was a great summer working with the youth at church and at camps.

We liked it so much there that we decided to make Calvary Temple our home base as we started on the evangelistic field that fall, traveling all over the Midwest and sharing God's message of hope. We were experiencing some amazing revivals, and God was opening doors and keeping us very busy. We found that besides a few short days here and there and the holidays, we weren't home very much, and when we were, we were far from our family back in Kansas.

It was now October, and Tamela started feeling under the weather; her vomiting had returned. I was preaching a revival in Coffeyville, Kansas, when she made an appointment to see a doctor to confirm she was pregnant. We were excited about another child; this put our children right at two years apart. But we also were aware of how hard pregnancy had been on my wife, and we were praying for it to be better this time.

It didn't take long for things to go downhill quickly with this pregnancy. Thanksgiving was just around the corner; we were at our home in Indianapolis. My wife was trying to decorate for Christmas, but she couldn't muster up the strength to complete the project; this was so unlike her. She was feeling exhausted; between trying to keep up with our sixteen-month-old and throwing up all the time, life was clearly taking a toll on her. To add to this, she was losing weight rather than gaining it, due to not being able to keep anything down, including water.

One night, she got up to go to the bathroom and passed out in the hall. Being a deep sleeper, I never realized she was gone. When she finally woke up, too scared to try to stand, she literally crawled back into our bedroom to wake me up and tell me what had happened. Shaken, I phoned some good friends of ours to come watch our son so I could take my wife to the emergency room. The medical staff felt she was just dehydrated because of the vomiting, gave her an IV with fluids, and sent her home, not believing it necessary to call an ob-gyn doctor in to see her.

We went home, only to wake up the next morning to find my wife's left leg was swollen to twice its normal size. She was in excruciating pain, barely able to put pressure on it to walk. I phoned my in-laws, told them what was going on, and took her back to the ER immediately. In the meantime, my mother-in-law caught the next plane to Indianapolis to help care for her daughter and watch her grandson.

When my mother-in-law arrived, my wife and I were still at the hospital. My mother-in-law knew something much more significant was going on than just dehydration, which is what the doctors and nurses continued to focus on. She began to question the hospital as to why they had sent Tamela home, considering that she'd been unable to hold down food or water for weeks. Why did they think only one IV bag was sufficient, and why wasn't she seen by an ob-gyn? Thank goodness, they listened to my mother-in-law, and my wife was finally seen by an ob-gyn, as well as an internist, and they immediately checked my wife into the hospital for further tests.

My wife spent several weeks, including Thanksgiving, in the hospital due to the blood clots that had developed in her left leg. These clots were caused by her getting so dehydrated from throwing up and not being unable to hold down any water. To get this under control, she had to start giving herself two heparin shots daily, to keep her blood thin and prevent more clots from forming. She was checked on a daily basis to make sure her blood level (INR) was staying in the intended range. Her blood needed to be thin enough to prevent more clots from developing or causing her to throw a clot, but her blood also needed to be thick enough to keep her from bleeding to death, which could have cost our child's life as well.

With her growing health concerns and the fact that we were on the road often preaching revivals, we decided it was best to move back home to Wichita, Kansas. We could base out of there and be closer to the family.

We put our belongings into a storage unit and moved in with my wife's parents until we found a place to rent. Shortly after our decision to return home, my wife's home church and Pastor Joe Voss—one of the pastors who had married us—started discussing the idea of me becoming staff evangelist at the church. This gave us a great covering, financially and spiritually, so we gratefully accepted the offer. It was a wonderful feeling to be part of a growing church that supported us as we continued to minister on the evangelistic field.

My wife's aunt and uncle had a house that they graciously offered us to live in for free; all we had to do was fix it up so they could sell it upon our departure. It was the house her uncle's father had built, and it had great character, but it probably hadn't been updated in forty-plus years. There were months of work to get the place ready and layers of wallpaper to scrape off; meanwhile, my wife was nearing her due date as we worked. Thankfully, we had some fantastic help from the people at church in getting the house ready.

We were ready to move in, but all our belongings were still in a storage unit in Indianapolis. We had left them behind because of my wife's sudden decline in health and our quick move back to Kansas to be near family.

Needing to get moved in and yet knowing the delivery was near made for a nervous trip. My good friend Marty Freeman (who played a huge role in my restoration later on) made the fourteen-hundred-mile round-trip journey with me in two and half days. My wife was still a few weeks out on her due date, but you never know for sure and that was the reason for our urgency.

We left feeling very grateful for being able to use my

wife's uncle's 1970s Chevy truck, averaging about seven miles per gallon, with no AC, no muffler, and pulling a cattle trailer behind to pick up our belongings. We left super early that morning and drove straight through. After arriving in Indianapolis, we were supposed to have some help from people at our old church, but unfortunately days or times got mixed up, and no one was there to help load except for me and Marty.

As Marty and I were beginning to unload the storage unit into the trailer, we realized all the big items were at the back of the unit and they needed to go in the front of the trailer to keep the weight in the front. We had no choice, so on a blazing summer day, with the sun beating down on us, we unloaded the entire unit and set it outside on the hot asphalt. After that, we started moving the large appliances into the trailer first and then loaded the remainder of our possessions.

We were finally done loading the trailer, and the storage unit was completely emptied and clean. It was getting late as we started the road trip back home, but we felt we could take turns and drive all through the night. But a little over an hour down the road, we realized that wasn't going to work; we were both exhausted from the drive and then having to unload and load our family's belongings. We stopped in Terre Haute for some much-needed rest. Waking up early the next morning, we started our trek back to Kansas, hoping to make it back in time to unload before the arrival, which we did.

Our second son, Landon, was born in June of 1989. Despite all the issues during the pregnancy, my wife's labor and delivery went very smoothly this time. We arrived at the hospital, she delivered our son, and then we were home in less than twelve hours, total. It was one of those moments, again, of incredible joy with a hint of sorrow. *I wish Mom were here, experiencing the joy of being a grandmother.*

Once Landon was born, we were thrust back into action

by preaching a heavy schedule that included summer junior high church camps in Kansas and Indiana. Handling a two-year-old and a newborn can be challenging, but there were plenty of younger girls at the camp who were more than willing to help my wife.

One Sunday evening, we had just arrived back at our cabin for the second week of Indiana camps. We were greeted with a note on our door to contact the district youth director ASAP. Naturally, a hundred things started running through our minds of what had happened! He informed us that my wife's grandmother had passed away, and the funeral was later that week.

As the guest speaker at camp, there was no way I could leave at this time. So, on Tuesday, a lady from the camp took my wife and our two sons to the airport. Tamela had to fly solo with a two-year-old and a four-week-old baby. While making last-minute flight arrangements, we were told we only had to purchase a ticket for my wife; the boys could fly free unless the plane was full. In that event, my wife would have to purchase a seat for our oldest son or find someone to hold him on the plane.

Thank goodness, the Lord goes before us and is always faithful. As it turned out, the plane was full on the second leg of the flight. With our money already extremely tight, purchasing another ticket would have been a huge blow. But God had already provided a wonderful older couple to be standing nearby the ticket counter when my wife was told the news that there wouldn't be a seat for her two-year-old son. In the midst of her sheer panic, the couple graciously volunteered to hold Dake on the flight to Kansas, and in God's perfect plans, He had placed them in the seat directly in front of her.

CHAPTER 8

The Early Years

THE NEXT THREE YEARS were spent traveling, with my family, as a full-time evangelist. We witnessed some amazing miracles, people getting saved, and powerful altar services during our travels. We met so many godly Christians and deeply devoted pastors who inspired us.

We traveled in a Ford Aerostar minivan. Car seats were not required at this time. Because we were in the vehicle so much and had two young children, we took the middle seat out so there was more of a play area for them while we were traveling. With the current laws today, that never would have happened! But it worked great for us on our long trips, and God kept us safe.

In the summer of 1990, I didn't have any meetings booked, so I took a three-week job with a custom combining crew to help us financially. I joined the crew in the Wichita area and traveled through WaKeeney, Kansas, and up to Ogallala, Nebraska, with them.

One day, I was running a John Deere 8820 combine near Wellington, south of our house in Wichita, and the clouds were getting darker by the minute. A few months prior, Hesston, Kansas, had been devastated by a tornado, and this storm had a similar feel to it. But I had learned from working on my dad's crew that you just keep cutting until the rain actually hits. Many times, it passes by without leaving a drop, and time not cutting means losing money.

The storm pushed to the north of us, and we never stopped cutting. We may have been out of the storm, but north was the direction of my wife and boys. I was listening on the radio for updates and kept hearing about the heavy winds that had hit Wichita—and trees and power lines that were down across the city—and I was growing more concerned for family. I was stuck in a field and had no way to get an update until later that night, so all I could do was pray for their safety.

They managed to ride out the storm in the basement of our home, with no real damage done to the house. There were several big limbs down and debris around the house, but everyone was safe, and that was the most important thing.

In the fall of 1991, our financial struggles continued. I was having another talk with God—and one that I'm not proud of. In Psalms 10:1, David says "Why, O LORD, do you stand far away? Why do you hide yourself in times of trouble?"

David knows God can handle the issue; it's more like he is puzzled that God hasn't responded already, that he appears to have kept His distance from the trouble David was facing.

I remember saying, "God, we are doing what You have called us to do, but we just can't make it financially." Then I made this arrogant statement: "God, I don't understand our financial struggles, but if You don't know how to provide for us, I know how to provide; it's called 'I'll go get a job.'"

I often look back and wonder how close we were to that miracle before I gave up. The heart of the problem was that I had failed to recognize and deal with a seed of doubt that had been planted when Jehovah Rapha (the God who heals) didn't heal my mother, and it was now manifesting itself in another area. *Maybe Jehovah Jireh (God who provides), who didn't heal my mother, is also a God who doesn't really provide.*

Sin and doubt are always a progression. Sometimes we think putting on the armor of God is just a great illustration, but the seriousness of the armor is shown when it only takes a crack in our armor to become a significant vulnerability. The small crack progresses to a large hole, making the armor useless. Putting on and maintaining our armor is not an option if we want to remain victorious!

A farmer understands that once a seed is planted, a sowing and reaping timeline begins to unfold. The Enemy is patient and unbeknownst to us lets the seed get deeply rooted before we ever see the manifestation of it. He patiently waits for his prime opportunity to strike and expose the doubt in our hearts. In hindsight, it's easy to see I failed to recognize the seed that had been planted.

In late summer, I took a job selling chemicals for a company. I continued to travel on Sundays and preach as much as I could, but I needed to do something to supplement our income. My wife was already working a part-time job that was offered by a family in our church.

In 1991, my wife became pregnant with our third child. After two complicated pregnancies, we were very concerned about the third one. But since the delivery had gone so smoothly last time, we felt excited and hoped that the worst was behind us.

After Tamela saw her ob-gyn, he suggested we needed a high-risk pregnancy doctor involved in her care, though he was still available to deliver our baby as he had done with our other two.

Our third pregnancy started out much better, and we felt this one might be different. Things had been going so well; Tamela was almost three months into it with no major sickness—just a little nausea from time to time.

She went on a trip with her parents to see the Kansas City Royals play—something she always enjoyed. It was toward the end of August, and it was hot. By the ninth inning, she decided to get some ice cream. Not long after finishing it, she had to run to the restroom, and the throwing up started again and basically never stopped. We thought, *Here we go again, day and night.* The vomiting triggered the blood clots and swelling in her left leg to return. This time it came back with a vengeance, and she was admitted to the hospital and placed under the supervision of a critical care pregnancy team.

The blood clots had stayed in her left calf in her second pregnancy with our son Landon, but this time they were moving up her leg. They had traveled up into her left knee, then to her left groin. The doctors were getting very concerned that if they couldn't get them to stop moving, the next stop in the path would be her lungs, which could kill her and the baby.

My wife and I, along with our church family, began crying out to God. After almost a month in the hospital, her clots finally got under control, and she was able to go home. The home care nurse, Faith, had to come daily to our house to monitor her blood (INR), as she had to resume giving herself heparin shots twice a day until the end of her pregnancy.

In December of 1991, I decided to join the family business in Great Bend, Kansas, and started as the general manager for my father's motel in January 1992. We figured this was just a pit stop in our ministry journey, one that brought some financial stability to us and a place we could get things in order and launch back into the ministry.

After my wife was on heparin for several months, she approached me and told me she felt God was telling her to trust Him for her healing and that she felt it was time to end the shots. This was at a time when I was taking my wife once a month to see her regular ob-gyn and every two weeks to see the high-risk pregnancy doctor, even as a nurse was coming daily to monitor her blood and make sure she and the baby were doing well.

Even so, I never questioned my wife; she's always had a keen ear to what God is speaking—and she wasn't one to claim God was telling her to do something very often. I told her she had my full support in whatever decision she made.

The next week we had our appointment with the high-risk pregnancy doctor, and my wife informed him that she no longer felt she was supposed to be taking the heparin shots. The doctor asked why. My wife told him she felt God was telling her to step out in faith and believe Him for her healing.

Now, I'm not telling you this story to encourage you to go off your medicine. To do something so extreme, I believe you must personally hear from God and only then take action based upon what He has spoken to your heart. You should never feel ashamed to receive help from doctors and medicines; God uses them to save people all the time. I share this story because I want you to see how God reveals himself when He has told you to do something and you obey.

The doctor looked at me and said, "Do you agree with what your wife is saying to me today?" I replied, "Yes." The doctor said if I wouldn't have agreed with my wife, he was going to recommend that she be put in for a psychiatric evaluation. He informed us that God didn't tell my wife to quit, and if she didn't continue giving the heparin shots, she and our baby would be in grave danger.

Needless to say, it was very frightening to hear what the doctor was saying. If I thought for one moment that God hadn't spoken clearly to my wife, we would have never taken that action. My wife and I had prayed about stepping out in faith and trusting God, and we both felt a sense of total peace about it.

As we started to depart the high-risk doctor's office, he stated that that it was the last time we could see him, and then he bluntly said, possibly the next time he saw us, my wife and baby would likely both be dead. That was a harsh reality, and the odds of survival were stacked against us.

Stepping out in faith always has its risk in the physical realm and often is not the popular thing to do. But when God speaks, you know you must act. Even so, the doctor's words echoed in my mind for days to come. *Are we doing the right thing? Did we really hear from God?*

The day before Valentine's Day, after nine hours of labor, my wife gave birth to a healthy 8 lb., 13 oz. baby boy, Darian. The nurse on duty that day was Faith, and the doctor on call to check out mothers once they had their babies was none other than our high-risk pregnancy doctor who'd said he'd never see my wife or baby alive again. I'll never forget him walking into that room, seeing her doing very well, and just turning around and walking out of the room without saying a word.

God brought both the doctor and the nurse full circle; my wife had told them she was trusting God to heal her so that God could show them how real He is and that He is on the throne and still in the healing business.

In March, we moved into a rental house that my father owned. It was in a small, older subdivision just outside the city limits. The house had been left in total disarray after the former renters moved out. For the second time in our marriage, my wife was nearing her due date, this time with our third child on the way, and having to help get a house ready and pack to move.

We had traveled full time ever since I had finished at Bible college. We never had a consistent income because we were totally reliant on offerings from churches where we were holding revival services, and then there were many weeks we had no services and no income. Now, having a steady income and a permanent home was a good feeling. We felt we might be there for a few years and then move back into ministry wherever God led us. As an added blessing, the boys were able to attend a strong Christian school that was only a mile away from our house.

As I entered the motel business with my dad, he was coming through a financially difficult time. Our community relied heavily on farming and oil, and both had taken big hits. This small-town farm boy, who had worked so hard and trusted God every step along the way, was in danger of his dream crashing. But he never quit giving his tithes and offerings, and he never stopped believing God for the path through this storm. By the time I joined him, things were tough, but the business was slowly on the rebound.

The restaurant, which had always done well, was now struggling with higher food cost and labor, and with the state of the economy, Dad could not keep moving the prices up at the same pace. My father had already defied the odds and been in the restaurant business for over twenty years. Seventy percent of restaurants that make it past the first year close their doors in the next three to five years. He said the restaurant helped him open the motel, and later the motel helped sustain the restaurant during that tough season.

My father and I attended a trade show in Minneapolis and stopped by the Perkins Family Restaurants booth to talk to them about the possibility of converting his restaurant. The talks went on casually for the next year, without gaining any real traction. Then, one day, corporate called and said they had someone who was interested in our location.

We were on the brink of the restaurant potentially ending its amazing run if something didn't radically change soon. But God already had a plan for His faithful servant. Enter Dan, who already owned the Perkins in Lawrence and Topeka. He and Dad became partners. They converted the Black Angus Steak Ranch to a Perkins and never looked back. This was an unbelievable blessing from God. Dad's restaurant has now been in business for forty-nine years. God defies all odds!

We were settling into our next season in life. Dake was in first grade, Landon in preschool, and Darian was growing rapidly.

Dake had tried different sports. He was a gifted athlete and he played through seventh grade, but it just wasn't his passion. His best sport was long-distance running, with a powerful sprint to close a race. I'll never forget a track meet where he was participating in the fifteen-hundred-meter race. About halfway through the race, he lost one of his shoes. I was on the infield watching him, and he lost it right in front of me. He glanced at me with a puzzled look, as if to say, "What do I do?" He kept running the next lap and a half with only one shoe, and he still put on an amazing finishing kick to chase down the person in front of him, finishing third. It was a great example of how he has approached life. Some things didn't go right—a "shoe" fell off—and he could have pulled up and quit, but instead he just kept running.

His real passions were riding an ATV (he only had one speed—fast), or trying to fix something, or going hunting. There's no way I could list all the things young Dake took apart that never got put back together correctly, but he always had to know how things worked, and as time went on, he started figuring out how to put them back together again. Little did we know at the time, he was developing his talent. He had a strong mechanical mind, and today he has a fantastic career using his mechanical know-how and is one of the top ones in his field.

Landon was a typical middle child; he was quiet, a homebody, and the peacemaker—the go-between—for his two brothers. But when it came to sports, he quickly excelled. He loved to compete. If there was a group of kids around, Landon came up with some type of game for everyone to play. His gift and intense passion for sports was clear, early on. When he was seven, he tried out in early spring and made a traveling baseball team for ten-and-under kids. He turned eight that summer but was thrown into facing kids almost three years older. But our quiet young boy thrived on the challenge.

Our youngest son, Darian, had a good mixture of both his brothers' traits. He was much like his middle brother, Landon, and excelled at sports; since he was with Landon all the time at all his sporting practices and games, he often played against kids older than him. It enabled him to have a "no fear" attitude when it came game time. Like Landon, he wanted to play baseball, but after signing with Manhattan Christian College, he was injured and ended his dream of playing long term. He also had traits from his oldest brother, Dake, and was blessed with a similar mechanical mind that enabled him to land in a great career to support his family.

I had the opportunity to start coaching Landon. The first team was a local recreational basketball program when he was in third grade. After the season, several parents wanted to start a traveling team, and so we formed one late that year and played one tournament against fourth graders. This went so well that we started a full-time traveling team the following year. This was an extraordinarily gifted class of young men. In basketball, from fourth to seventh grade, they never finished worse than third in the state tournament.

I started coaching many of these same kids in baseball, and during our travels, we met two coaches from the Wichita Cardinals in the district tournament: Galen Worley and David Dean. We faced them three times in the district tournament and defeated them twice to move on to the state tournament as district champs. Years later, Coach Galen joked with me that when his handpicked team from a large town was heading to Larned, Kansas, for districts, they were expecting to walk through and easily punch their ticket to the state tournament.

But they ran into an all-star team from the little-known town of Great Bend that played the game with great heart and a never-say-die attitude. Galen said to me, "How could we score over thirty runs in three games and lose two of three?"

Landon had a great tournament and caught the eyes of the Wichita coaches by closing out two of those games, and also with his hitting and his ability to play catcher.

The next year, I had the honor to coach his eleven-year-old Great Bend Mariners, which was made up of several of the former all-star team members. We played a challenging schedule and traveled a lot during that summer. Landon enjoyed being around his friends, but baseball was more than that to him: even at an early age, he knew he wanted to play professionally. He talked about it often. The coming fall, he gave up playing football to play fall baseball in Wichita on the weekends.

The following year, when he was twelve years old, we made a brutal decision to leave his friends in Great Bend and go play for the Wichita Cardinals. We felt, after talking with Landon, that playing at a very competitive level might be a significant step for him.

As a bonus, the Cardinals were going to play in the Cooperstown Hall of Fame Tournament in August of 2001, and that was just too great of an opportunity to turn down. In a small town, it was not the most popular decision but one we felt was best for him in the long run. Little did we know that Cooperstown would be our last big trip; we are so thankful for that moment in time and the memories it created.

The Wichita Cardinals played in the championship game of every tournament they entered that summer (except Cooperstown). We only missed a few league games during the season in Wichita. We traveled four hours round trip for him to play a league game. During this time, he met a great friend named Mitch Caster.

Darian played on his own teams, but he also suited up for his brother's games and was able to fill in for us as a pinch runner. The first tournament of the season, we were playing our rivals, the Cubs. With the game tied, our pitcher had just gotten a hit but wasn't very fast. Darian was blessed with speed and had great baseball smarts for his age. We subbed him in to run for our pitcher. He stole second base and then third base, eventually reaching home on a passed ball. We won our first game against our rival.

Life seemed to be cruising along and bringing much fulfillment along the way. We felt very blessed, even though I was running from the call of God on my life, we were creating some great memories with our family. Great Bend really was a nice community to raise our boys in; we have wonderful family and friends still there today.

Around 1995, we decided to upgrade our dated manual property management system at the motel front desk and modernize to a computer system. I began the search and ran across a user-friendly system that was just starting up. We installed this in our motel, and we became a beta-testing property for them.

This also opened the door for me to become a dealer with the company. I traveled to motels to install the hardware, as well as to train desk clerks on the software. I installed over twenty systems in motels. We were blessed when the company needed to send a trainer to Canada for three weeks to help prepare a group installing the system on their own in seven of their motels. The paycheck for that was a huge boost.

This opened the door for me to open a computer store in 1998. Looking back and understanding so much more about business now, we were clearly undercapitalized and never really had a chance to make it without the needed cash flow to buffer the early days.

But this leads to a major regret for me. A good friend invested in us and partnered in this venture. When things go south, money and time are lost, but friendships are by far the most enormous cost. Business is never worth the price of a good friend. In the midst of other things going great, this was a significant setback and one that still tugs at my heart because of the loss of a friend.

CHAPTER 9

"Your House Is on Fire!"

IT WAS A TYPICAL HOT, WINDY DAY in late June 2000, and we were in the first game of a scheduled doubleheader. The ball fields were located in the middle of a cell phone dead zone.

One of my assistant coaches, Brad, who was also a sheriff's deputy, called time-out and began walking from our first base dugout to the third base coaching box, where I stood.

It was like everything was in slow motion as Brad walked toward me. Something was up, but I had no idea what could be wrong.

The sheriff's office had been unable to reach him by phone, but they were able to reach him on his pager, and he went to a location with cell phone range and called dispatch. He calmly said, "You need to go; your house is on fire."

What? I don't remember the next few moments very well. I was trying to grasp the shock of the news while imagining our house and all our belongings being destroyed.

I found my wife, and we quickly took off on the ten-mile drive to get back to our house, leaving the boys with friends. The drive seemed to take forever.

Curiosity didn't kill the cat, but curiosity about kept me from getting to my house. As we came to our gravel street, there were so many cars in the road wanting to see what was on fire that the road was blocked, and no one was moving. Fortunately, I had a truck, and I was able to pass some cars by driving partially in the ditch, and then I was able to cut across our vacant field to arrive at our house in time to see the fire department had the blaze under control.

The south side of the exterior looked to be intact, as we approached from that direction. But as we got out of our car and headed toward the front, we could see the damage. There was a big hole in our roof near the front door, which is where the fire had started. A faulty outdoor porch light was later determined to be the cause of the fire.

We were blessed that a neighbor saw smoke coming out of an attic vent and called the fire department. They, then, were able to contain the fire and rescue our animals that were inside; the fire chief said that another five to ten minutes and the house would have been leveled, but most of the structure was intact. Now the smell of smoke and ashes from putting out the fire was everywhere inside.

Days later, the insurance adjuster kept insisting that they only needed to repair a few rooms where the fire did the most damage. My wife, who has a very keen sense of smell, kept saying, "That isn't good enough; there's smoke in all of these walls, I can smell it."

The adjuster told us that eventually it would air out. My wife knew better and took a hammer to the Sheetrock one afternoon, in the room farthest from the point of the fire. Once she ripped a hole in the Sheetrock, there was little argument; you could see the burnt edges of the insulation and a realization of just how close we were to the whole house being consumed. There was no argument now; it was clear that smoke damage was everywhere, and the house needed to be gutted. The damage ended up being over $90,000, and it was considered to be a total loss. Over the course of the next four months, our family of five lived out of a motel room while our house was being repaired.

When I share my testimony and all the things we have been through, I generally don't share this because, in the scope of things we suffered, this wasn't that bad in comparison.

There is little doubt that having a house totaled is a severe trauma to endure and a frightening thought. We felt that devastation. But let's put this event into perspective. It was just a house, and the contents were just things. Losing a home is no comparison to the finality of losing a loved one. Or the finality of being sentenced to prison and losing invaluable time with your family. Things can be replaced, but we never get to add time to a life that was taken too early.

My mother had written in her diary about using time:

> When the children were younger and in so many things, I was beginning to get weary from all the driving to and from their activities in one day. The Lord showed me what a blessing these times are, along with my kids or when you're alone in the car—no TV, no telephone, no neighbors driving by. Just you and your kids. You have a chance to communicate. And I begin to look at it as quality time alone with my family. I learned so much about them.

Too often we put the emphasis on things and the speed of life cause us to miss crucial opportunities to value the time we have with our children and family. Even every car ride has value. There are no guarantees of how long life will last. But we must slow down, cherish every moment, and redeem the time.

CHAPTER 10

Takotsubo: Broken Heart

THE PROPHET JEREMIAH DESCRIBES the devastation of a broken heart: "My joy is gone; grief is upon me; my heart is sick within me" (Jeremiah 8:18). The NLT translates it this way. "My grief is beyond healing; my heart is broken."

Takotsubo is defined by Harvard Health as "a weakening of the left ventricle, the heart's main pumping chamber, usually as the result of severe emotional or physical stress, such as... the loss of a loved one...That's why the condition is also called stress-induced cardiomyopathy, or broken-heart syndrome."[1]

Medical News Today further explains it in their June 28 letter. This horrific medical condition as well, saying, "Takotsubo is a grieving surge of abnormal electrical waves that causes the heart to deflate and contort until it resembles a fishing pot. Hollow and cold, an empty vessel at the bottom of a fathomless sea."[2] We were about to experience all of this and more.

---

1 "Takotsubo Cardiomyopathy (Broken-Heart Syndrome)," *Harvard Women's Health Watch*, Harvard Health Publishing, November 2010, updated April 2, 2018, https://www.health.harvard.edu/heart-health/takotsubo-cardiomyopathy-broken-heart-syndrome.

2 *The Blacklist*, season 4, episode 12, "Natalie Luca (No. 184)," directed by Michael W. Watkins, written by Noah Schechter, aired February 2, 2017, on NBC.

Life was on cruise control. The family was doing well, and we were making enough money to be able to do fun things. But the cruise control was about to malfunction, the brakes to quit working, and life to speed straight into a black hole that would forever change our lives.

Our local high school football team had struggled over the recent years, but a new young coach from Texas was changing the culture to a winning tradition and bringing excitement to the community.

On October 19, 2001, Great Bend was playing a crucial game against Salina: this game most likely would decide who made it to the state tournament. The energy at the stadium was at an all-time high. It was loud and raucous. Later, we were told about the hush that came over the stadium as the news spread.

I was leaning on the fence near the goal line, on the south side of the stadium, when my phone rang. It was my dad. I thought that was odd, but I figured I'd better answer since Dake and Landon were at his house.

They loved going to the Friday night football games, probably not so much for the game as to hang out with their friends. But they were out of school, and the two had spent the day at Grandpa's house. They were having so much fun out in the country, riding four-wheelers, that they didn't want to quit playing to go to the game.

I answered the phone and heard the words no dad ever wants to say to his son: "Rick, there's been an accident, and Landon may be dead." Nothing in the world can prepare you for those words.

All I remember is yelling in the phone, "NO!" My wife was by my side, and although I hadn't had a chance to officially tell her, by the look on her face, she knew something had gone horribly wrong. We took off running to find our nine-year-old son who was playing with his friends. Deciding not to take him until we knew for sure what was going on, we found our friend Brad, the sheriff's deputy, and his wife Laura and told them what had happened. We asked them to watch Darian and took off running to the car.

We left quickly, with the hazard lights blinking, racing to the scene of the accident. Landon and his oldest brother had been riding their ATVs back from a friend's house around dark, and Landon had somehow come off the flood dike and run right into a barbed wire fence with a support bar running across the top. We were told later by the doctor that it was instant.

My fourteen-year-old son, Dake, was with Landon. He was on the lead ATV, with Landon's friend Joe on the back of his seat. When he looked behind him, he quickly knew something had gone wrong; Landon's ATV was not on the dike. He raced back to the ditch, only to find his brother lying on the ground, unconscious. He took off to find Grandpa.

Joe stayed at the scene, while Dake raced to get help. I can't even begin to imagine what was running through Joe's young mind. My heart breaks for him and what he had to experience that night also, and he is in our prayers still to this day.

As my wife and I neared the scene, we could clearly see the sheriff's and ambulance's lights in the distance. I pulled off the road and without even thinking, we both entered into action based upon how God designed us as a father and mother.

Being the man—a protector—and wanting to see how I could fix this nightmare, I ran toward the ambulance, only to be denied access by the officers and told that things didn't look good. From a distance, I could see my son strapped into the ambulance with paramedics working on him. My wife—showing her mother's heart to nurture and love a child in need—went to find Dake, to hug him and Joe and try to bring them comfort in a comfortless situation.

There are no adequate words to describe the rest of the

night. There are no words to describe what my oldest son and Landon's friend had just witnessed. The night was a blur as we headed to the hospital, praying for a miracle.

We entered the hospital to see my aunt Cherine working at the check-in desk. She has described that night as the worst night of her life, as she sat there helplessly watching events unfold. We sat in the waiting room, crying and praying. Finally, the doctor came in and gave us the official news that Landon was gone and that we could go see him if we wanted to. We mindlessly walked back into the ER and looked at his lifeless body and just wailed. All that came out of us was a deep groaning and flood of sobbing emotions. We couldn't even speak, but then again, there just weren't any words to describe the gut-wrenching reality you are experiencing in such a moment. It was every parent's worst nightmare.

We left the hospital with broken hearts and the foggy realization that it was over. All the time praying, *Please, someone, wake me up from this nightmare. This can't be happening.*

We now had to go get our nine-year-old son and somehow try to explain to him that his brother Landon was gone. That his brother and roommate was not coming home ever again.

It's hard enough for an adult to try and make sense of this tragedy, let alone our fourteen-year-old son, Dake, and our nine-year-old son, Darian. As a parent, your heart is ripped out with your own loss, and on the other side, your heart is ripped in shreds, knowing what your sons will be left to deal with.

We took Dake and Darian home, and when we arrived at our house, there were several close friends waiting for us in our driveway and wanting to do their best to console us. I started making a few calls to family and some close friends, but in a small town, the news was traveling like wildfire.

Two of my closest friends since grade school, Marty and Randy, drove from Wichita to sit with us until early in the morning and then returned home. Tragedy and tough times will quickly show you the depth of your friendships, and we were truly blessed with great friends. Everyone knew that consoling was an impossibility, but they still wanted to be by our sides.

My wife's parents and her brothers also arrived that evening to attempt to console us, with my family flying in the next day. My wife spent the night sitting and walking around the outside of our house and the baseball diamond we had built for practices, reflecting on so many memories of Landon and the boys playing. I decided to try to lie down with Darian. Landon and he had shared a bed, and he did not want to go into the room and sleep by himself, so I took him to our room and laid down with him. The night was restless and seemed endless. I couldn't stop tossing. I decided to go sit on the floor of our walk-in shower and just weep while water was running over my head; it felt like my tears were matching the water from the showerhead in a constant and endless flow. Was this real? Once again a wail arose from deep inside me, reminding me how real it was. I thought to myself, *I sure wish I could talk to my mom right now or just get a hug and feel her comfort.*

Darian never was comfortable again in the room they shared, and Dake, being the older brother, once again showed a big heart and switched rooms with his brother. It couldn't have been easy for Dake to go into that room either.

The next morning, we prepared to go to the funeral home to start making funeral plans. It's such an awkward situation and feeling. There you are, sitting around a large table, trying to make plans and decisions about the funeral; it almost feels like you are conducting some type of business meeting. All you really want to do is go hide, and in your mind, you're still trying to grasp if this is even real. You want to cry, but by now, you have already cried so much that tears are hard to come by, so you just feel numb as you sit at a table making final arrangements.

Food, food, and more food kept arriving at our house, one visitor after another showing their support and love. Tamela's uncle, aunt, and cousin from Arizona had taken a bereavement flight to be with us, and other family members also flew in. Friends and family were a pleasant distraction from the constant thoughts of how we were going to survive life without our son.

Tears and laughter rarely cross our minds as things that happen at the same time. But there we were, laughing and crying from one story to the next. We laughed talking about the good times and shed many tears from our crushed hearts that there would not be any new stories to share. Our memories were now the entirety of the life we would live with our son.

The funeral was set for Tuesday.

A big part of my time with our boys was taking them hunting. The weekend before, Dake, Landon, and I had been in our hunting boat out at Cheyenne Bottoms. It was a windy day, and the waves were splashing over the bow. I was at the rear, driving, and I was staring at them with great joy and laughter. These were priceless times for us. I watched them stick their heads up just above the top and then duck just in time to miss the splash, laughing at each other every time it happened. Oh, how quickly laughter can turn to tears in life.

We got set up: at the end of the boat, there was a platform, and it was easier to shoot from for a smaller person. Dake was on the platform, and Landon was beside me, pouting and complaining about not being tall enough to shoot over the boat blind quickly enough. Dake, being the typical older brother, would concede to Landon and let him have his way, switching spots. He wasn't necessarily happy about it, but that's what big brothers do. Great memories.

Now, in the midst of our own dark despair, our top concern was for our remaining sons.

It may seem odd to some that the day before the funeral I chose to go hunting with my son. Despite my own grief, I was also consumed with finding ways to help our boys. My wife and I decided I should take Dake hunting on Monday. It's what we loved, and it's how we spent so much time together.

I woke up that morning, and there wasn't a bone in my body that wanted to go hunting. I sat on the edge of the bed by my wife, with tears streaming down my face. "I just want to go back to sleep and not think about this," I said. She kept encouraging me: "You need to go. Dake needs you. This is important."

The hunt that morning was one of the calmest I had ever witnessed. It was a weekday, so there weren't any other hunters out. There was virtually no wind, which is really odd for Kansas, and there was a dense fog. We could see about twenty yards in front of us. We could hear the ducks flying and quacking around us, but thanks to the fog, we couldn't actually see them until they were close to landing in our decoys.

Two worlds clashed. In the physical, there was this unbelievable calm and surreal setting I was physically sitting in. But on the inside, my heart felt like it was in a war zone that was about to explode, screaming, in the horror of what we were facing, the looming question: *How will we survive?*

Dake and I were able to talk about Landon and reminisce about some of the great hunts we all had shared and some other special moments. Before we loaded the boat to go home, we both rose, raised our guns, and in unison, gave Landon a three-gun salute from one of his favorite hunting spots.

We left that calm morning to be thrust back into the reality of final preparations for the funeral and to more visits from friends and family.

Another restless night passed, and Tuesday morning arrived—time for the funeral. Pastor J. P. McCamey and

Pastor Joe Voss who had both married us and dedicated Landon to the Lord as a baby officiated the funeral.

I have no idea how many people were there, but the sanctuary could seat close to one thousand, and it was pretty packed. The community was out in full force.

Landon's teammates from the various teams he had played with over the years wore their jerseys to the funeral in honor of their teammate. Several teammates had signed balls for us, and the Wichita Cardinals brought their large league trophy from the past summer to give to us. People were extremely thoughtful in helping us honor our son. Landon wore his baseball uniform as he was laid to rest. His favorite sport. #30 gone forever.

I mindlessly watched people walk through the line to say their final goodbyes. All of a sudden, I saw Glen, the head referee for our tournaments. We had become good friends. He had watched Landon play many basketball games over the years. I watched him as he paused, looking at my son lying in the casket, took a slight step backward, and raised his arms to signal one last time a made three-point basket. A signal he had made for Landon probably hundreds of times through the years. This little thing brought a small smile to my face in the midst of a dark day.

He told me later that he signaled that because he always got a chuckle out of Landon. Whenever it was time to end warm-ups and come to the bench to start the game, Landon was always the last one there because he had to make one more three-pointer. Glen said to me, "I signaled that at the casket to represent my memory of him and that I know he made one last three-pointer on his way home, and to signal the memorable impact he had on my life."

The service ended, and we headed to the gravesite to say our final goodbyes before our son was lowered into his earthly resting place (not his spiritual resting place). All the while I was still thinking, *Someone please wake me up from this nightmare. This can't be happening.*

His grave was next to my mother's. I thought to myself, *She finally got to meet one of her grandchildren.* I knew he was in good hands, but that's little comfort for a broken heart.

A few weeks before Landon passed away, Tamela came home from a stressful day at work where probably nothing had gone right. I'm sure she had walked into a house terrorized by three boys and that just added to her stress. Instead of taking it out on the boys, though, she walked outside and sat on the front porch to cool off. Landon could tell Mom had had a tough day and sensed her frustration, so he went out on the porch and sat beside her. With his gentle spirit, he put his arm around her and said these simple words: "It's going to be okay, Mom."

I've often imagined that Landon was looking down from heaven, rooting for his family to survive without him. Putting his arm around us and saying, "It's gonna be okay, guys; just hang in there."

CHAPTER 11

Triggers

OUR NEW REALITY. The dreaded phrase I mentioned in a previous chapter now took on a much deeper and darker meaning: "Life goes on."

Really? Because it sure doesn't feel like it. There is little question that life is moving past us when we are lost in grief, while we seem stuck in the moment, stuck in perpetual takotsubo, a dark hole of hopelessness. Life has come to a crashing halt, and there appears to be no future. In our minds at this point, life doesn't go on.

How would we move forward? Where would we find hope? Our world was crushed, and although we hoped for a brighter day, we knew that part of us died that day with our son. C. S. Lewis explains it this way: "The death of a beloved is an amputation."[3]

Job 5:11 says, "He raises up the down-and-out, gives a firm footing to those sinking in grief" (MSG). It feels like the grieving process is endless sinking. But though we will always grieve, we can find firm footing in Christ.

It is very easy to become consumed with our grief. Dr. Larry Crabb says, "The grieving process for me is not so much a matter of getting rid of the pain, but not being controlled by the pain."[4] The pain wants control; the pain

---

3 Madeleine L'Engle, foreword to C. S. Lewis, *A Grief Observed* (1961; repr., New York: HarperCollins, 2009), 6, Kindle.

4 Larry Crabb, quoted in "Day Four—Grief Lasts Longer than Ex-

wants to blind us not just to a brighter future but to any future at all.

Every time I thought I was taking a step forward, I fell two steps back. Triggers are difficult to understand if you have never lost a close loved one. You will be having a good day, and then, out of nowhere, you run across a picture of the one you lost, the baseball field where he played, the first park you took him to, birthdays, holidays, and especially the anniversary date of his passing. And with each trigger, our mood quickly turns from feeling okay to dark.

Sometimes it's a trigger you don't even recognize at first. My wife was used to buying our milk on a set schedule. One day, she realized we were wasting milk; the last several times we had purchased it, it expired before we used it all. She paused to think about it, and all of a sudden it hit her and a flood of emotion came out of nowhere. Landon was the big cereal eater. He was the early bird, and we always knew when he was up because of the sound of clanking bowls in the kitchen. What we would do to hear those bowls clanking around in the morning again!

Life doesn't feel like it goes on; it feels more like a ship in a bad storm, being tossed up and down from one major wave to the next, with no lifeboat nearby and no end in sight. *Why fight? Why go on?* are the looming questions.

My friend Dr. Terry Yancey explains grief and triggers like this: It's like you put on a one-hundred-pound weighted vest. The weight is overwhelming at first, but over time you start to get used to it. But you never get to take the vest off. You will forever carry it with you. Just when you are getting used to it, you move too quickly, and its weight about knocks you over.

Finding consistency in our emotions seems almost impossible. We find our self on a good day, only to be knocked

pected," Grief Share, accessed May 22, 2019, https://www.griefshare. org/dailyemails/recipients/zDx45LngQnva8OrUmRwT/messages/4.

down by a trigger; we scratch and claw on the next day to find some semblance of happiness, only to have triggers knock us down again. We get weary of the ups and downs and searching for that elusive solid ground.

C. S. Lewis, in his book *A Grief Observed*, written after the death of his wife, Joy, explains it this way:

> For in grief nothing "stays put." One keeps on emerging from a phase, but it always recurs. Round and round. Everything repeats. Am I going in circles, or dare I hope I am on a spiral?
>
> But if I spiral, am I going up or down it?
>
> How often—will it be for always?—how often will the vast emptiness astonish me like a complete novelty and make me say, "I never realized my loss till this moment"? The same leg is cut off time after time.[5]

James Bruce, in his book *From Grief to Glory*, shares the story of Hetty Wesley, sister to John and Charles, who lost three children. Bruce's reflection on Hetty's loss masterfully paints a picture of what grieving and triggers are like:

> Hetty says "Real grief is not easily comforted. It comes like ocean waves rushing up the sand, subsiding back, only to roll in again. These waves vary in size, frequency, and intensity. Some are small, lapping up around the feet. Others are stronger; they foam the water around you and cause you to stagger. Then there are the overwhelming waves with an undertow that can turn your world upside down and drag you out into the deep water. In times such as those, the mourner desperately needs an anchor. And, indeed, God has promised His people a blessing if they patiently endure. He has guaranteed the promise so that we might lay hold of the

5 C. S. Lewis, *A Grief Observed*, 69–70, Kindle.

hope set before us. This hope is the anchor of the soul, and it is sure and steadfast (Heb. 6:19)."[6]

We had great people surround us and stand by us, but soon everyone had to get back to their own lives. When this happens, you feel like you are left in the middle of a vast field all by yourself—no one around, no place to hide, no distractions; just you and your new best friend, grief, trying desperately to find comfort for your takotsubo.

One day I was sitting in my backyard having another conversation with God:

> I just want this pain to go away, I want our lives back the way they were. But deep down, I know it is a vain request. Life will never be the same, and we will forever carry our loss. God, You sent some supportive people to surround us and offer comfort, but they all get to go home. Their lives go back to normal, and they get to kiss their kids goodnight, but I'll never get to kiss my son goodnight again, and I'm having a real hard time understanding a God who allows this to happen. Maybe You aren't the God that heals, maybe You aren't the God that provides, and maybe You aren't the God of love, because how can that be a God of love?

The seed of doubt that was planted now manifested itself in full bloom.

It was a dark moment, a vicious spiritual attack, to the point that I even wondered if life was worth it; maybe it was time to just check out. I felt a dark, hopeless cloud swarm all around me, like there was no way to move forward—and if you can't move forward, is life really worth it?

Shortly after losing Landon, I made this statement to my

---

6 James W. Bruce III, *From Grief to Glory* (Crossway Books, 2002; repr., Carlisle, PA: Banner of Truth, 2011), 70.

oldest son, Dake: "I've already lost one son, and I don't want to lose another one," meaning that I didn't want him to go down a path of self-destruction that would make me lose him. Yet, there I sat in my backyard that day, with hopeless thoughts swimming around in my own head.

Those words I'd spoken to Dake served as my own wake-up call and a reality check for myself. I had to be strong; I had to figure out a way to move forward. No one can even begin to understand what Dake faced the night of Landon's death; he was only fourteen. He could have easily chosen a path of self-destruction—and on one hand, who could blame him? No young man should have to witness what he witnessed that dreadful night.

That day in my backyard, I realized that if I gave up my sons most likely would follow suit—and that meant life would basically be over for them. If my wife and I didn't lead them through the super difficult journey ahead, that might thrust them down a potentially long and dangerous road, letting their hurt drive them into deeper and darker places and eventually to a point where there was no escape. This would lead to their lives never being productive again, to them always hiding behind the pain of their loss and making it their excuse for not really living life.

Tamela's and my focus had to be on our remaining two sons. We had to live out by example that dreaded statement that *life goes on*. In our deepest hurt, in our times of feeling like giving up, the love we had for our two boys was a driving force that kept us moving forward; even if it was at a snail's pace, it was progress in the right direction.

Trying to lead the boys and trying to make sure we didn't lose our marriage in the process was challenging. Grief is very difficult on a marriage. It's hard to be on the same page at the same time because grieving has its own timetable, and each individual is drastically different. Also, men will grieve much differently than women, and it's easy to think if someone doesn't grieve like us, then they aren't grieving at all.

James Bruce explains the complicated journey for parents and helps shed light on why so many marriages struggle during this time. He writes:

> What lies beyond the cemetery is the valley of weeping. Even before we leave our child's grave, we have begun the journey into that valley. Only, we don't know how deep or how extensive the valley is, and this can make the descent both sad and fearful. Worse yet, if we are married, our spouse will also be in the valley. And though we enter together, we may not stay together. Often, one spouse will take a different path and, perhaps, go to places lower than the other can follow. Thankfully, there is a faithful Guide, a Good Shepherd to lead us through the valley.

James Bruce goes on to quote Robert Dabney, a theologian who suffered the loss of a son and two weeks later lost another one: "This is the first death we have had in our family and my first experience of any great sorrow. I have learned rapidly in the school of anguish this week, and am many years older than I was a few days ago."[7]

The school of anguish is a school no one wants to attend. We can be sent to that school for a hundred different reasons, from bad decisions to becoming addicted to yielding to depression. But the loss of a child is final, and that school of anguish has no end.

We were about to face our next lesson in this school, as the holidays were fast approaching. How could we survive? Our family sat around the Thanksgiving table, attempting to be thankful—but thankful for *what*? Our hearts and minds were consumed with the empty chair at the table. It had just

7 James Bruce III, *From Grief to Glory*, 48.

been a little over a month. How could it not consume us?

Our next lesson from the school of anguish was lurking just around the corner—Christmas. Rather than stay in Great Bend, we decided to go visit family in Arizona. My mother always made Christmas so special, and I was blessed with a wife who was just like her when it came to holidays. But how do you make such a Christmas special? The usual anticipation was replaced with a feeling of dread and heartache at just the thought of celebrating Christmas without our son. Once again, we had Dake and Darian to think of, but we struggled with what to do for them. How could we salvage an important time celebrating the life of the King who was born to save the world when our hearts were broken by the life we had just lost.

Going to Phoenix—having family around us and being in a different place—helped make it somewhat more bearable. Distractions are never the permanent answer, but there is little doubt that they help us waddle through those early days and years of grieving.

My wife started a great tradition that year—one that we still practice to this day. She bought a gift for Dake and Darian from their brother Landon. The gift was one that he would have likely given or one that fit his personality.

With mixed emotions, we watched the boys open each gift, fighting back the tears and grasping to find the joy in this season. But as hard as we tried, joy was clearly elusive. This Christmas brought back thoughts of my first Unmerry Christmas when my mother was released from the hospital for a few hours to be with us. My thoughts drifted again to wishing she was there to help us walk through this tragedy.

CHAPTER 12

Healing through Coaching

I HAD HAD THE OPPORTUNITY to coach Landon's baseball and basketball teams since they were in the second grade. This was an incredibly talented class; in high school, they won back-to-back state championships in basketball, played in the state championship game in football, and made it to the state baseball tournament.

Not only were they great athletes, but they were great young men. It was fun to be a small part of their lives.

After the accident, I remember telling Greg, Cecil and Scottie, my assistant coaches, that they were going to have to take the basketball team over. "I just can't face it right now, not in my state of mind," I said. They completely understood and offered their full support.

But as a little time passed, I realized those boys had been like sons to me. I desperately wanted to send Dake and Darian the right message about life. What kind of message was I sending them by quitting? I wanted to send a simple but painful message: "Life isn't fair; life will throw all of us some big curveballs, but how we respond to them is what is really important."

I decided I had to live that example out, not only to my family but also to Landon's friends. Instead of hiding in a shell—which was my top choice, based upon how I felt—I needed to force myself back into action. I agreed to coach the boys for their last season together before junior high. I walked into the gym for the first practice of the year, trying so hard to be strong for everyone, but the flood of emotions was inevitable.

This was the same gym where I had spent so much time with Landon, where we often stayed after practice to play H-O-R-S-E or to work with him on an aspect of his game, where he worked on that last-second half-court shot. It was a place where I had previously felt so much joy watching his passion for the game. There were so many great memories with all the boys in this place. But there was no joy in the gym that day; it was filled with sadness, and it was clouding my ability to focus on the present. I was stuck in replays of our past in this gym.

Most of the parents attended that first practice to show their support and appreciation, but no one really knew what to say. Even though no one knew what to say, often just being there is saying enough. When we try to comfort someone who is grieving, we always think we have to say something profound and comforting. In reality, many times all a grieving person really needs to know is that we are there with them and maybe even willing to shed some tears with them.

I'm reminded of a story my good friend Pastor Bobby Massey told me. Bobby's family owned a Grade A dairy. He was just finishing the fourth grade when he was pulled out of class and taken to the car where his siblings were. They were all crying, and he had no idea why. He rode home in silence to his family's farmhouse, only to be told that his oldest brother had died in a tractor accident that morning. He was in shock and disbelief, trying to grasp what he had just been told. But at 3 p.m., as Bobby recalls,

> my dad said, "It is time to go get the cows; they still have to be milked." They were approximately a quarter mile away from the house in the north pasture. As I was

walking around the barn to head up into the pasture, a friend from school appeared, walking around the other side of the barn. He was in the seventh grade and had come to the house with all the other families to bring us food after hearing my brother had been killed that morning. When he approached me, I asked him, "What are you doing here?" and his reply was profound: 'I didn't think you should walk alone today.'"

Bobby said they went to get the cows, and he doesn't remember another word being said while they were bringing them in, adding, "I have no clue if he even remembers doing that, but it meant the world to me."

That is a powerful example of what we so often need when we are grieving. We just need to know we aren't walking alone. Just being there says so much more than words could ever say!

Over time, practices became more bearable, but every time I walked into that gym, it was a constant reminder—just like the empty chair at our house—there was an empty uniform, a missing team member.

The boys wanted to do something to honor their teammate, so they put my son's number on their shorts and created a warm-up T-shirt in honor of him: a panther paw, with his number 33 in the middle of the paw.

These boys had never finished worse than third in state and had been runner-up several times. We had one nemesis: McPherson, the only team it seemed we could never beat. Their coach and I, despite our intense rivalry, had become good friends. The entire McPherson team showed up for the funeral in their uniforms, and they had all signed a basketball to give us. Several weeks later, we played our first tournament, and of course, we drew McPherson for our first game.

What happened before that game was one of the classiest

acts of sportsmanship I have ever witnessed. McPherson, our rivals, pulled off their warm-ups, and every player was wearing a wristband with my son's number, 33, on it—and they wore these all year. They presented me with a gift, and each player gave me a hug before the game started.

Fighting tears as the game began, I was trying to remain strong, but I was an emotional train wreck on the inside, and the next hour was a blur. I don't remember very much about the game. All I really know is that we suffered one of our biggest loses ever as a team—and who could blame the boys? I was coaching without my son, and they were playing without their teammate against one of the state's top teams.

I remember sitting them down in the hall after the game and having a heart-to-heart talk about what had just happened and what we wanted our future to be. I only used the Landon card twice that year. Once was after that game, and once before the start of the state tournament.

I'd always preached to them, that win or lose, we would play the game hard and never back down from anyone. "I understand we all faced conflicting emotions today when we played," I said. "I know you saw a coach that was coaching with takotsubo, a broken heart. Landon isn't with us anymore, but we will not change the way we play the game. I'm coaching you all because of my love for you guys and my son, but we will play the game the way he played it. We will play with passion, and we will leave it all on the court."

Driving home, I reflected on one of the last basketball games I'd coached Landon in, at the state tournament. We got up for our first game, and he was feeling sick. Tamela and I debated about even sending him to the game. Maybe he should rest and just get ready to play the next day. But he was adamant that he wanted to go.

He lay down in my truck and slept most of the way to the game. He barely participated in warm-ups, but he begged to start the game. I agreed but let him know if he wasn't up to par, I would have no choice but to rest him and hope he was better by Sunday. He responded by playing his heart out and leaving it all on the floor. He was the leading scorer for that game and went on to be the offensive MVP for the entire state tournament.

The boys were true champions at heart, and they responded to the loss in that first tournament by winning all their games and making it to the championship game. That also meant a rematch with McPherson in the championship game. We lost in a close game, but it was a bitter battle to the end, and it sent a powerful message. We may have been broken, but we would not quit. The boys left their hearts on the floor that day, with an outstanding effort. I was so inspired by their effort. I drove home that day thinking about Landon and how proud he would have been of the way his friends had just handled adversity.

We met McPherson several more times that season and always knocked on the door of victory but could never get over the hump. This was leading to a classic state championship matchup. For only the second time that year, I talked about doing this for Landon. I pulled out his jersey, and we laid it across a chair on the bench. "Let's win state for Landon!" I said. We led for a big part of that game and lost it coming down the stretch. In the midst of a loss, my heart swelled with pride once again at how they had battled during that game. There was no quit in these young men.

We entered our last tournament as a team, the MAYB (Mid America Youth Basketball) season finale. We finally beat McPherson for the first time ever in a hotly contested semifinals matchup. Perseverance—never quit—was always our theme, and the team clearly proved it was more than just a slogan.

The reward for that great win was that we got to play another dominant team, the Wichita Backyard Players. This was my last game to coach these amazing boys, and it was only fitting that the underdogs—a team from a small town named Great Bend—were facing a giant from Wichita (similar to our beginnings in baseball) and won an exciting game in double overtime. What a way to go out!

It was such a fitting way to end. They had started the year in grief. They refused to give up, and they dug deep and battled all season to push themselves to the next level, and they ended with two of the biggest wins in a row they had ever had, rewarded by being crowned champions. It was more than a trophy; it was a life lesson. It was a lesson that no matter what life throws at you, you can make it.

The season that started in a cloud of grief but ended in a celebration of joy and perseverance. Although my intention was to be an inspiration to the boys, they became an inspiration to me.

After the basketball season, I accepted the opportunity to coach Darian's baseball team for the first time; he was ten at the time. It was a great experience to be able to finally coach him, and he was also surrounded by some classy kids.

It's easy to hide when life gets tough. I know firsthand what it's like to just fade into the background. But one of the most powerful healings that came to me was by facing that hurt head-on and trying to stay involved.

Maybe the greatest destruction grief can bring is in keeping the focus on our pain and brokenness. Sometimes, even though we don't feel like it, we need to get out and serve others, get outside our comfort zone, and this starts shifting the focus off of our pain.

The focus on my family and those boys helped me reach outside of my takotsubo, my broken heart, and start to comprehend that saying I never liked to hear: "Life does in fact go on." It was time to rejoin it.

CHAPTER 13

The Dedication

PEOPLE IN OUR COMMUNITY rallied together and approached the city about naming a baseball field after Landon. They attended a city council meeting, and the council agreed to change a field to Landon Tate Unruh Memorial Field.

In April, we had a stone sign put up that had his baseball picture engraved in copper and these following words inscribed in it:

> Outside of God and family, Landon's greatest love on this earth was playing baseball. Landon played his first competitive baseball game on this field when he was 7. Landon continued to excel in baseball until his untimely death at age 12. His love and dedication to the game was amazing. Landon accomplished a lot in his short 12 years. At 10 Landon played in the Hap Dumont World Series in Springfield, MO where he would hit a home run. In the state playoffs, Landon pitched a perfect game. When he was 11, in the USSSA World Series in Kansas City he pitched a no-hitter.
>
> In the fall of 2000, he decided to give up football and play fall baseball to continue to improve his game. Landon was a true "gamer." If the game was on the line, he would find a way to make something happen. The bigger the game, the more he seemed to excel.

In August of 2001, he played in the Cooperstown Dreams Park World Series in Cooperstown, New York where the Major League Baseball Hall of Fame is located. At the end of the tournament he was inducted into the Youth Baseball Hall of Fame. In the fall of 2001, I had Landon write down his goals and dreams for his future. He dreamed of playing college baseball and then going on to play in the major leagues.

It is the hope of Landon and his family that every person who steps onto this field will play baseball with the same love, passion, sportsmanship and intensity that Landon played with, and if you do, one day you will be able to fulfill the dream of a little 12 year old boy named Landon Tate Unruh. Through hard work, determination, and God's grace all dreams are possible.

We planned a field dedication and an opening ceremony in April. We gave away the first Landon Unruh Memorial Scholarship to a baseball player from our local area who was going to our community college. This first recipient was Matt Hafner, who had developed a friendship with and been a mentor to Landon. Multiple people shared their memories about Landon, and Pastor J. P. McCamey gave a short message and prayer of dedication. Dake and Darian both had the honor to throw out the ceremonial first pitches to finalize the dedication of their brother's field.

We also had a time of sharing. One of the stories was told by Landon's Wichita Cardinals coach, David Dean. He used an example that happened on the very field we were dedicating. It was a great story that really summed up Landon's drive and instincts for the game. He was a competitor.

It was a scoreless game, there was a leadoff walk, and Landon was up to bat. The coach gave him the bunt sign, which did not happen very often. He laid down a well-placed bunt that moved the runner into scoring position at second. The next player singled, making the score 1–0.

Two innings later, the opposing team had a runner on third, with no outs. Coach Dean called a time-out and walked to the pitcher's mound. Surrounded by all the infielders and Landon, the catcher, he said, "We can't allow a big inning, so we will let that run score at third on an infield ground ball and make sure we get the out at first. We will trust our bats and pitching to win the game later."

The other team decided to call a safety suicide-squeeze play. The batter bunted the ball to the side of the pitcher. He reacted quickly and fielded it clean. Coach Dean smiled as he retold this part of the story: "All I remember is Landon, our catcher, frantically calling for the ball at home plate, all the while I'm yelling to get the out at first." The pitcher heard Landon hollering and made the throw to home, Landon blocked the plate beautifully, just like he had been instructed. We waited with anticipation for the umpire to move around to the front of the play and check to make sure Landon still had the ball in his glove; he then signaled while yelling, "You're out." He went on to say that Landon had a gift and great instinct for the game, and those two plays summed up his ability to do whatever it took. The Cardinals went on to win 1–0. Coach Dean later jokingly said, "I love it when a plan comes together and the boys make me look good by following my exact instructions."

Scott Graham, another baseball coach from McPherson who had become a good friend, was present that day also and spoke about how Landon would join his team when he wasn't playing with his home team. Since Landon's death eighteen years ago, Scott Graham has called every year on his birthday and on the date he died. He doesn't have to say much; just the fact he remembers says more than you can imagine to someone who is grieving: "I know today is a tough day, but I just wanted you to know that Karen and I were just talking about Landon and remembering what a great kid he was. We just wanted you to know that we miss him and are praying for you both today." I know the call is coming every year. For eighteen years, it's been predictable and still moves me to tears when I simply see his number on my caller ID.

CHAPTER 14

The Pursuit of Happiness

C. S. LEWIS SAID: "I sometimes wonder whether all pleasures are not substitutes for Joy."[8]

I felt that getting a new start might be good for us. My father wanted us to stay in Great Bend. He had worked hard to build his businesses, and it would mean a lot to pass it on to family, but he also understood and was completely supportive of our need to move on.

In August 2002, I left the family business to pursue a career in the mortgage industry. My sister Shawnda had been very successful in the mortgage business, and she helped open the door for me to get an interview with a manager for the central region. The only opening they had was in Springfield, Missouri. My wife had strong reservations about the move, but she had always been supportive and decided to make the most of it. We were leaving the security and comfort zone we had enjoyed in Great Bend. We were leaving behind some terrific friends and family, and some great memories. We were also leaving behind the memory of our worst nightmare.

Dake and I moved first, into a rented duplex in Ozark, Missouri, so he could get started in school in August. Tamela stayed back in Great Bend with Darian until October, to keep our health insurance until mine kicked in with my new job.

Darian was in the fourth grade, and it is always a little

8 C. S. Lewis, *Surprised by Joy* (New York: HarperCollins, 1955), 209.

easier to move, the younger you are. As a sophomore in high school, Dake had a tougher time with the move. Not to mention, it was less than a year since the boys had lost their brother.

My new job in the mortgage industry was in a brand-new territory with no existing clients. It was going to be sink-or-swim situation. I was leaving a consistent paycheck and moving into a commission job as an account manager. I had no clue about anything to do with mortgages; ironically, I was supposed to be teaching mortgage brokers about our products and how to structure a loan package to be submitted to us.

My job was to build relationships with mortgage brokers, teaching and coaching them about our guidelines to get them to submit their loans to our company. The challenge was huge, and in some ways, maybe I needed that to push me out of my comfort zone—to keep me focused on something new, which meant less time to focus on my takotsubo.

I have often heard people who have suffered a loss say that they think about their loved one every day. That used to seem hard to imagine, until it happened to me and I learned firsthand that a day rarely went by without the thought of our son.

The mortgage business was booming, and I dove right in, motivated to be one of the top reps in the company. I quickly gained a foothold in the market and started developing some great business relationships.

My wife took a part-time job at Dillard's and found great success. She was the only part-time person to make the presidents club for sales at their store. She had a gift in helping people, and they responded well to her honesty and recommendations.

Money started flowing in, and I quickly learned something: that money can buy happiness. It became a great distractor from reality. People are always searching for happiness. Do a quick search for "happiness" in Amazon books, and you'll find more than forty thousand results. That's a lot of people writing about happiness—and, presumably, a lot of people looking to find it.

By definition, happiness conveys the idea of chance or luck. One dictionary defines happiness as "a pleasurable or satisfying experience."[9] Aristotle is summarized by saying, "Happiness is a state of activity."[10]

Darrin McMahon writes, "It is a striking fact that in every Indo-European language, without exception, going all the way back to ancient Greek, the word for happiness is a cognate with the word for luck. *Hap* is the Old Norse and Old English root of happiness, and it just means luck or chance, as did the Old French *heur*, giving us *bonheur*, good fortune or happiness. German gives us the word *Gluck*, which to this day means both happiness and chance."[11] We can have moments of happiness based on circumstances, but such happiness is unsustainable, because those activities, chance, or luck will disappear.

On the other hand, joy is sustainable when it is solely based upon what Christ did for us. Joy is not based on events or circumstances. It is based on the fact that Christ died for our sins, and no matter what happens, that can never be changed.

Happiness is an up-and-down experience, always based on chance or luck, with things going on around us spiking that emotion.

Joy, on the other hand, is more like rolling hills. It is more

---

9 *Merriam-Webster*, s.v. "happiness (*n.*)," accessed May 22, 2019, https://www.merriam-webster.com/dictionary/happiness.

10 *The Nicomachean Ethics*, Trans. J.A.K. Thomson (London: Penguin, 2004), PG 15, 16.

11 Darrin M. McMahon, "A History of Happiness," *Yes!*, October 1, 2010, https://www.yesmagazine.org/happiness/a-history-of-happiness.

consistent. The only way to find true joy is to find it in Christ. You cannot fake joy—you either have it or you don't.

Joy is mentioned in the fruits of the Spirit's indwelling in us: "Love, joy, peace, patience, kindness, goodness, faithfulness, gentleness, self-control" (Galatians 5:22–23). Paul prayed for the church at Rome, "May the God of hope fill you with all joy and peace in believing, so that by the power of the Holy Spirit you may abound in hope" (Romans 15:13). In Christ, the believer can "rejoice with joy that is inexpressible and filled with glory" (1 Peter 1:8).

We see Paul live this out in his life. Paul and Silas knew adversity, as they sat with their feet in stocks in a prison cell. Their legal rights had been violated. They had been arrested without cause and beaten without a trial. At midnight, since they couldn't sleep, they sang joyously the praises of the Lord (Acts 16:25). A miracle soon followed (verse 26).

Adverse circumstances destroy *happiness*, but instead of hindering our faith, they can actually enhance our *joy*. James wrote, "Count it all joy, my brothers, when you meet trials of various kinds, for you know that the testing of your faith produces steadfastness. And let steadfastness have its full effect, that you may be perfect and complete, lacking in nothing" (James 1:2–4).

Since Satan can't create real joy—one that is based upon Christ and the Holy Spirit—he can only create moments that emulate joy. *Happiness is Satan's counterfeit to what God wants us to experience in joy.*

I learned that money could buy distractions, it could provide moments where I could feel happy again, where life seemed temporarily normal and the pain was subdued. I could buy the latest technology, take nice trips, buy new vehicles, purchase a new house. It all seemed great at the time, but it eventually wears off. It was only a temporary cure and one that always left me looking for the next high. I was addicted to money as a means to find some sort of happiness.

Our one-year lease at the duplex was coming to an end. In September of 2003, we moved into a beautiful 2800-square-foot home, and it seemed like we were making traction. *Maybe life does go on*, I thought.

Dake's junior year was a very difficult one. The move had been tough on him. Sometimes I wonder if it was the right thing to do, and yet, Springfield is where he met his beautiful wife who eventually gave us three incredible grandkids.

Dake and Darian battled through some very tough times in dealing with the night of Landon's death. But today I am super proud to say that despite what life threw at my sons, despite having every reason to just quit, they have persevered and overcome. They now are working in the same field, and both have become very successful. They are my heroes, an inspirational story of what can happen when you don't give up.

Darian had quickly made new friends and was asked to play on a traveling basketball team. After basketball, they were looking to put together a baseball team and asked if I had any interest in coaching them. It was a great honor to coach a talented bunch again. They went on to be state champs as eleven-year-olds and runners-up as twelve-year-olds. Darian was fitting right in.

A friend had started a mortgage-consulting company, and we decided to purchase a newer, bigger home through his company. Looking to create new avenues of happiness and becoming discontent with our nice home, I wanted more. In February of 2006, we purchased and moved into an amazing 4400-square-foot home. Later, this decision came back to bite us.

Then, continuing to try to cure the ache in my heart, I bought a new truck and bought my wife a used Jaguar. My thirst for happiness was unquenchable—and unsustainable. I couldn't afford to keep buying new things; unbeknownst to me, the mortgage crash was fast approaching.

Money was flowing in, but it was flowing out just as rapidly. There wasn't much room for error. In late 2006, the mortgage industry began to collapse. By early 2007, it was an out-of-control freight train. It seemed like almost every day lenders were going out of business.

Everything was collapsing around me. We had two rental homes: the one renter who was paying decided to move, the other I couldn't get to pay rent, and I couldn't even afford my own mortgage. With no money and things falling apart, I could no longer support my addiction to happiness through money.

It was during this time that I cried out to God and surrendered the life I had made a complete disaster of. It's sad that it takes us getting so low sometimes before we look up. Yet we can be thankful for those times that draw us back. In my pain and questions about God and how this could happen, I had tried to find my own ways to mask the depths of darkness deep inside of me, but to no avail. It's only a hole that God can fill.

We had never really tied into a church when we moved to Ozark, but we started attending a local congregation again and seeking God's direction in what we were dealing with. The church had a prayer room open, and many a morning I began my day there, seeking God's help. Slowly, I started feeling the call of God stirring upon my life again. But deep down, I felt too broken to ever be used by God.

In the midst of the mortgage industry crashing and our own financial crash, I heard the first whispers that the FBI was in town investigating mortgage fraud. On one hand, I wasn't too concerned about it since we clearly felt everything was aboveboard. That being said, just the suggestion of the FBI checking into anything you are involved with can spark great fear, because they don't mess around. We immediately ceased moving forward with any new deals until we saw what unfolded with the investigation.

CHAPTER 15

Roadside Encounter
with God

IN MAY OF 2007, we decided to start over once again and move back to Wichita, Kansas, to be closer to family and friends.

We started attending Believers Tabernacle, a church pastored by my friend Pastor Marty. The pastor and church played a massive role in helping relaunch me into ministry, and they stood by me when many churches would have distanced themselves.

I moved back to Wichita unemployed and frantically looking for a job. Through my previous contacts in Missouri, I interviewed and was hired as a regional manager for a start-up mortgage company. This seemed like a great opportunity, and our fresh start was gaining traction.

Three weeks into the new job, I had not received a paycheck but had received a lot of empty promises on when I was going to get one. Meanwhile, they already had me traveling to different towns in my region to look for places to open offices and to interview potential loan officers to work in these offices. Not only was I not getting a paycheck, but I had incurred additional traveling expenses, and none of those were being reimbursed. I started getting a sick feeling that the potential dream job was going to be a bust. Sure enough, within a month or so, I was unemployed again. The company launched before fully being funded, and the funding source fell through. Now I had added more debt from my travel expenses and lack of paycheck.

I renewed my search for a new job, finally accepting a sales position for Renewal by Andersen, selling windows. This was stressful because it was 100 percent commission, but it was also gratifying work. I loved the people I was working with and loved meeting customers. God was faithful and granted me great favor.

The call to ministry that had been on my life, which I had successfully squashed into some dark corner for many years, was slowly reviving itself. It eventually became a consistent thought and prayer for me. *God, what is your plan for my life?* I prayed. *I know I may need more schooling, or I may need to do some other things to prepare for it, but if you will just show me, then I'll have that goal to look forward to, and I can start working toward it.*

There had been complete silence from God concerning my purpose in life. On the one hand, my personal devotional life was terrific, and I was hearing from God often, but when it came to that question of what His plan was for me: silence. I knew deep down, though, that He still had a plan for me, and for whatever reason, I wasn't ready for it to be revealed.

Time went on, and I was growing more and more frustrated by the constant silence. It crept into eighteen months of continually asking God to reveal His plan, and still nothing. I was becoming frustrated and baffled by God's silence. I needed to understand my purpose in life. We are always looking for the quick answer, but God's timing is perfect, and He knows when we are ready for that next step.

One day, while driving north on I-135, heading to my next sales appointment, I was having the same conversation with God about what my purpose and calling was in life—and the growing frustration that I didn't know.

Out of the blue, I heard His voice: "You should have been dead." It rattled me for a moment, it was such an abrupt comment out of nowhere, and then I heard it again: "You should have been dead, but I still have a plan for you."

Immediately, He took me back to something I hadn't thought about in a long, long time. Darian's baseball team in Ozark had agreed to travel to Great Bend to play in the Landon's memorial tournament in early April. A good friend, Kenny Smith, had kept the tournament running in honor of our son. There are no words to express our appreciation for all his hard work and what that meant to us.

The boys played their pool play games that day and prepared for the single elimination on the following day. Saturday night, I was up and down all night, vomiting and not getting much sleep. The boys lost their first game, and we were ready to leave early that afternoon to head back to Ozark. By evening, we were on Highway 71, heading south to Carthage, Missouri. Growing up on the farm, driving vehicles for ten to fourteen hours a day was something I was used to and had done many times. I had driven all over the US as an evangelist and never ever remotely came close to falling asleep. But with the emotions of the weekend, the lack of sleep due to feeling sick, and the dehydration, I had fallen asleep at the wheel. I woke up just as we were driving into a grass median separating the traffic, and I instantly thought to myself, *There's nothing in front of me; don't slam the brakes!* But it was too late because I was already reacting by stomping on the brakes and turning the wheel back toward the road. This threw us into a spinout, going around multiple times. Tamela and Darian were in the car with me, and they had both been asleep but now were wide awake in an out-of-control spinning car.

As we were sliding on the grass, we were nearly horizontal as we were about to slide onto the asphalt. When something is moving fast on a slick area, and the tires hit something firm going sideways, the tires will grip all of a sudden, and the momentum normally leads to a rollover situation. I braced for it; I knew it was coming. I literally felt the side of the car starting to lift. I thought, *This is going to be bad.* My life flashed before my eyes. *This may be the end.*

Miraculously the car did not roll, and we spun out back across the highway and came to a stop on the bank in the ditch. People were stopping to pull over and check on us. Everyone was okay, the vehicle was fine, and we were able to simply drive on down the road. Nobody had much to say—all of us recovering from the shock in our own ways.

I knew my life was spared that day, but with God now whispering a gentle reminder, I broke out into instant worship and was encouraged to know that God wasn't done with me yet. He did save us that day, and He did have a plan, and He would reveal it in His timing.

I continued onto my sales call with renewed hope and confidence that God's plan for my life was still intact. "Just be patient, just be patient," I kept whispering. I made a nice sale that night. Icing on the cake.

Over the years, I've visited with several people who know God has something big in store for them, and they are frustrated that He hasn't opened the door. I always ask, "What are you doing for Him now?" It's easy just to sit back and wait for that big moment, the big promise. I always encourage people to get involved *doing* something, instead of being stagnant in serving others while waiting for the big reveal.

Tamela and I remembered that after we had attended a large church in Ozark, the next day we had a knock on our door from a member bringing some cookies, some information about the church, and a map of the facilities. They wanted to know if they could answer any questions and pray for us. It made a memorable impact on us.

In the midst of me waiting desperately to hear what God's big plan for us was, we decided to start a cookie ministry at our current church. My wife baked the cookies, and we took off on Monday evenings, driving all over Wichita, delivering cookies to people who had visited church the day before. In the process, we met some great people. One of the men we met became a good friend and to this day will still call me "the cookie man" when he sees me.

We wanted to continue to serve in any way we could, so when the pastor asked me to become part of the teaching team for our discipleship class, I thought it wasn't my final calling, but it was better than sitting on the sidelines.

One particular evening, I shared some of our story about losing our son and about God's hand on our lives and how we were blessed to be part of the church. Even with the loss of our son, I could clearly see that God had brought us there. My openness led to others opening up about some deep things they were battling in their own lives, and it turned into a powerful moment of people sharing their hearts and the Spirit filling that room.

After teaching that class, despite the positive interactions that had occurred, I sat down and suddenly began to feel overwhelmed that maybe the end might be near. Maybe trouble really was lurking around the corner as I had heard more whispers of an investigation. If so, my life and call to ministry could be easily destroyed by the FBI investigation. *Why am I even wasting my time leading this class? I may be facing probation or jail time, and God could never use me then.*

As I sat sulking about a potentially bleak future, God spoke to me. He said, "You can look back, and you can clearly see how I have gotten you from point A to B. You just testified to the class about how clearly you see my hand guiding your life. But now you are struggling to trust my plan and my ability to get you from point B to point C?" This hit me like a ton of bricks. *Okay, God, I have trust You no matter what. You have proven yourself to be faithful, and*

I know You still have a plan for my life. Your plan will be fulfilled; I just wish I knew what that plan looked like.

In the fall of 2008, I was driving to my next sales call in Hutchinson, Kansas. As usual, I was having the same conversation with God: *What is my purpose? What is my calling?* I was passing through Colwich, Kansas, when I heard what seemed to be an audible voice: "You haven't given Me everything."

I pulled the car over in a parking lot, and honestly, I was in disbelief. *What? In case You haven't been paying attention, Lord, we have pretty well lost everything, and we are starting over. I don't think there is anything else I can give You.* I can assure you that you probably don't want to make that statement to God!

He said, "You haven't given Me everything; you haven't given Me your son."

Ouch. *Oh no, not going there. I've tucked that away in a closet, locked the door, and thrown away the key; there's no way I am going back there. I've worked very hard at covering up my takotsubo. I still have a lot of questions about how You could allow these types of things to happen to people, and especially to our son. Behind that locked door is nothing but pain and confusion.*

I sat in that parking lot, as tears started streaming down my face, and I replayed that statement in my head over and over again: "You haven't given Me your son." After some time passed and with much hesitation, I mentally saw myself picking up my lifeless son, sobbing with each step as I walked him to the foot of the cross, laid him down, and said, *Okay, God, here is my greatest hurt in life, my deepest wound, and some of my biggest questions about who You even are. But if You can use my son for Your glory, I'll do whatever You ask me to do.*

Instantly, after eighteen months of praying and tirelessly seeking my purpose, it begins to rapidly unfold. God began to flood me with His plans for my life. The "Dream Again" name immediately came to me; I had never remotely thought of that name—or any name for that matter—because I had no clue what ministry I might be called into. "Dream Again" could apply to so many things that people have gone through that have stolen their ability to ever dream again. For me personally, it applied to me losing my son. When that happens, you never think you'll dream again; you never think you'll understand passion again, because all you can feel is numbness and pain deep inside.

In the scope of life, what do winning and losing have to do with anything? Though I am a highly competitive person and never want to lose at anything I play, I tell people I would lose every game I played for the rest of my life if it meant I could have my son back. In my brokenness and hopelessness, I felt I would never feel real passion or excitement again. I had resigned myself to the fact that I was going to walk around like a robot for the rest of my life, merely going through the motions, always stuck in that tragic moment in time.

But God steps in, and He does restore our dreams, and He does restore the purpose for our lives. I realized I could feel alive again—never forgetting the past but using it to begin to help others.

I'll never know for sure why it took eighteen months for me to find my calling, but God always knows best, and evidently, I hadn't been ready to self-surrender my deepest hurt and pain. That could have continued to be a stumbling block to me if I had just launched into ministry without truly dealing with it.

When I surrendered my deepest hurt in life—my son—
it unlocked the door for me to dream again.
Self-surrender is the key to discovering
God's plans and dreams for us!

I immediately called my pastor and set up a meeting with him to share my experience. After discussion and prayer, we decided to open the Dream Again Counseling Center, using a vacant office at the church. I would use my tragic experience as a backdrop to help those who were grieving, battling addictions, feeling hopeless, facing marital issues, and so many other problems. The message was this: No matter what you are facing, no matter how hopeless it feels at the moment, God can repair your life and bring you new hope. God can deliver you from your addictions and offer you a new and lasting high. For those grieving, it is going to be a long journey, but if you stay the course, God still has a plan.

I started researching ways to get training and decided on Logos University to get my bachelor's in Christian counseling because of their strong belief in a biblical counseling strategy. Since I already had attended Bible college, I had close to one hundred credits that transferred. I basically just needed to take thirty credit hours in counseling classes.

In the midst of this, my wife started experiencing increasing issues with swelling and pain in her leg. She had had a few instances of pain since the pregnancies, but they always went away fairly quickly. For example, flying home from a business trip to Hawaii in the late 1990s, my wife felt excruciating pain in her leg. She tried to walk around the airplane and stretch her leg. It was a long flight, and there was no relief in sight. But when we landed, all the pain disappeared fast. Since it went away so quickly, we didn't think much about it. In hindsight, it should have been a warning sign to us that she was having clotting issues again.

While we were living in Missouri, she occasionally got pains in her groin area that caused her to walk with a slight hitch in her step, but again, they generally went away after a few days, and we didn't think much of it. She must have just aggravated a muscle or joint. But it was another ignored warning sign.

Roughly sixteen years after her last pregnancy blood clot issue, we were thrown another twist. Although I had a job, it did not provide insurance. But her leg started swelling. She was trying to wait it out, thinking it would go away like it had in the past, but deep down, she knew this one was different. These symptoms were very similar to what had happened during her pregnancies. Because she has Native American heritage in her bloodline, she had an Indian Health Card. This allowed us to go to Tahlequah, Oklahoma, and take her to the hospital's emergency room at no cost.

Similar to what we experienced in Indiana, the emergency room did not feel this was a significant issue. This was like déjà vu. My wife was persistent; she knew what this felt like, and she knew it was serious. They just wanted to give her an IV and do an X-ray and send her home. Finally, after much pleading from her, they agreed to do an ultrasound on her leg.

After a few moments, the puzzled ultrasound tech asked her, "Have you had surgery before on your veins?" Tamela was surprised by the question and answered no. They never told us how many clots she actually has in her leg but referred to them as "a lot."

A main deep femoral vein that delivers blood back to the heart was totally dried up, due to old blood clots. But God intervened and did His handiwork to keep my wife alive. The reason the ultrasound tech had asked the question about surgery was because she told us later that it looked like a doctor had done surgery to repair her vein and helped reroute the veins to keep blood flowing. She said, "I have never seen anything like this without surgery being involved." God was my wife's surgeon that day.

The hospital staff realized she needed to be on blood thinners ASAP. They immediately administered her a shot of Lovenox, which is a synthetic version of heparin—a blood thinner—but her body had an allergic reaction to it that caused a severe rash and major itching. They decided to switch her to heparin, a drug that they knew she wasn't allergic to since she'd used it previously, and put her on a prescription of Coumadin (an oral blood thinner) for the remainder of her life, as she was diagnosed this time with chronic deep vein thrombosis (DVT).

Having multiple blood clots all through her left leg caused her to walk with a limp. That threw her entire body out of alignment, and soon her other knee hurt worse than the leg with blood clots. Backaches and migraines all intensified over the years after this incident. One thing led to another and the pain spread throughout much of her body. She's tough and not one to complain. She birthed three healthy boys with no pain meds, after all. So when she is vocal about her pain, you know that it is bad.

By May 2009, I had finished my degree, and the Dream Again Counseling Center launched. It was an indescribable day. All we had been through, all our hurts and wounds, all those questions would now be used for God's glory to help other people walk through their trials. I had found my purpose! I didn't have any clients yet, though, so I continued to work part time and was going to offer counseling a few days a week. I set up my office that day, and I didn't want to leave, the presence of God was so thick. There was such a remarkable anointing in that place. Just reflecting on God's goodness and that He always has a plan for us, I thought, *Now I get to live out my purpose in helping others.*

I wish we were closing this book and celebrating this moment; I wish everything finally went back to normal at that point, but another major setback was just around the corner—one that felt like it was going to be the final takedown.

The Enemy loves to wreak havoc on our mind and

thoughts, because that's the door to hopelessness: the end-less cycle of discouraging thoughts that lead us downward. I would come to feel like I was just doomed to be defeated. My views became tainted, and I almost feared the moun-taintop experiences because it felt like nothing good lasted for me. Being on the mountaintop only meant there was a valley coming. The mountaintops were short-lived and the valleys felt endless. Life was nothing more than one bad thing after another happening to me.

CHAPTER 16

The FBI

ABOUT A MONTH AFTER we opened the counseling center, I get a call from an unknown number. Normally, I don't answer unknown calls, but this was the third in two days, so I decided to pick up. It was an agent with the FBI, and they wanted me to come in for questioning about a marketing/consulting group I was involved with.

As mentioned previously, in early 2006, I purchased our home through a friend's marketing company. He had come up with this marketing/consulting company as a way to purchase a home, and he had been operating for a year or so before I joined. Later that year, I had heard rumors that the FBI was questioning some of the home buyers involved, and that was eventually confirmed when a couple that I knew informed me they were interviewed. That scared me enough that I immediately ceased doing any more deals through the marketing/consulting group. A few months later, I was told the couple who had been interviewed was looking to hire a lawyer. This was alarming news. I became very concerned and expected to be called in at any time to be interviewed. But it never happened. In May of 2007, we moved back to Wichita, Kansas, we had not heard anything else about the investigation for close to two years.

I was staying focused on what God was calling me to do. I had pressed full steam ahead in finishing my Christian counseling degree and opening the counseling center.

Needless to say, I was completely caught off guard when I finally received the call that day.

The agent asked me to come down the following week to be interviewed about my involvement. *Here we go again—coming from a high to crashing halt*, I thought. *Is this really happening? Oh well, it's just an interview.*

While my friend had set up the marketing/consulting group with the advice of an attorney, there was still some hesitation on my part about whether it was operating legally or not, but after watching deals get closed and seeing more real estate agents get involved, I started thinking about getting involved too.

The day I was convinced this was a legal company was when I started looking for a new house. I planned on using the marketing company for the purchase. Tamela and I found a beautiful home that we fell in love with. I found a builder who had a home nearly completed, and visited with him; he was also a real estate agent working for a large firm in southern Missouri. He said he had to check with the real estate broker and see if they were okay with using my friend's company's marketing agreement for the purchase. He came back a few days later and said that their team and lawyers were okay with the marketing agreement, and in fact, several other agents had already been involved with previous transactions through the marketing company. At that response, I felt very confident that this was a legitimate agreement, and it was safe to proceed.

There's always such a fine line when admitting to something, to avoid shoveling blame. When someone offers an apology and then follows it with a "but"—with a list of excuses to justify their behavior—instead of just fully admitting their wrong and moving on, the apology loses its meaning. "I am sorry that I hurt you, *but* you know I just had a bad day," "*but* you know how angry that makes me when you say that, "*but* . . ." Instead of just admitting we were wrong, without a list of excuses that caused our reaction, sometimes we try to justify our actions or place the blame on someone else. This is a personal struggle in how I address this next part of the book.

I take full responsibility for my actions and have paid a heavy price for them. The marketing agreement was proven to be illegal, and I clearly participated, and I accepted my punishment and did my time. So, do I end there or add a "but" to explain things?

Instead of defending all the reasons we felt it was legal, the only things I will address are my mindset, what we were told at that time, and my heart. We were told the agreement was legal, and we never set out to intentionally defraud anyone: I can say that with a clear conscience. My greatest mistake was something the FBI said to me multiple times: "Did you personally hear a lawyer say it was legal?" or "Why didn't you hire your own attorney to get his opinion?" And they had a valid point. I should have hired my own counsel to get their interpretation.

The old adage is "If it sounds too good to be true, it probably is." That's pretty strong advice to live by and probably could have kept me out of this mess.

Money had become my path to happiness, and the marketing company allowed us to make more money, which led to more temporary happiness for me. The bait of happiness was my driving force, bypassing any alarms going off in my head initially that this company and concept might possibly be illegal.

Real estate agents are bound by many laws and a code of ethics. For them, the idea of giving a rebate on a house is clearly illegal. It was presented to me by my friend, who started the company, that the marketing/consulting company was not under those same restrictions. They were simply marketing the property and consulting the builder. They were using real estate agents to handle the actual sales transaction. The builder had a right to hire a marketing company, if he chose to, and they were not under the same laws as real estate agents and could offer the rebate.

This concept was designed somewhat like a wholesale club. Being able to sell more product at a reduced price, and, in the long run, actually making more money.

The marketing company found buyers and had them ready to purchase each home as soon as it was finished. This allowed the builder to keep his cash freed up—no utilities, no property taxes, and savings on the interest he normally had to pay while waiting for the property to sell, which could potentially take months, adding more expenses to his bottom line. Since it sold right away, the builder could move onto the next project immediately and not have any additional expenses.

Therefore, the builder could afford to sell the homes at a discounted price because he didn't have to cover long-term expenses from the houses not selling quickly and keeping utilities on, paying taxes, and so on. This meant, he could sell more homes at a smaller profit per house and still come out ahead at the end of the year.

The marketing company received a fee for their service. The agreement was clearly shown on the closing papers, and the title company cut the check from the proceeds of the loan directly to the marketing company to cover their marketing/consulting fee.

Real estate agents were involved in the overall transaction to cover the legality of the sale. Houses were sold at the top end of the appraised value, and to my knowledge, none of the appraisals that I was involved with were unfair. Most lending companies have a thorough appraisal review process, and on many occasions, because of the sales price of the home, it automatically triggered the lending companies to send out their own appraiser to verify the value or at least trigger an additional internal appraisal review. Those almost always came back within range. Upon closing, the marketing company took out their fee, and then the balance was rebated back to the buyer.

It was presented to us that that the federal government could not control what the marketing company did with their funds, and the marketing company was not under the same regulations as real estate agents and so could rebate money back to the buyer.

It sounded like a legitimate loophole, but that statement alone can be the heart of the problem. When we are looking for loopholes, there are too many variables and too many ways to fall off course—and loopholes are always open to someone's interpretation.

Many Christians live their life in a similar fashion, always looking for loopholes instead of seeing what we can do or give up to draw closer to God. Why do we often look for those loopholes and try to figure out how to keep our relationship with God too, while walking a fine line with the world's standards? The loophole says, "Lord, what can I *keep* and draw closer to You?" The surrender is, "Lord, what can I *give up* to draw closer to You?"

When it came time for the FBI interview—and I never would recommend this for anyone else—I went without a lawyer. I had prayed about it and felt comfortable with my decision and just laid it all in God's hands, trusting His promise that He had a purpose for me. He had miraculously helped us get the counseling center open, so I thought, *He's got this. If I'm guilty, I'm guilty.* If so, I believed for God's favor in the sentencing process. I was trusting His plan for my life would be fulfilled.

I left early that morning from Wichita, for the nine-hour round-trip drive to Springfield. I entered the interview room full of uncertainty and anxiety. There were three agents on one side of a large conference table, two were with the FBI, and one was an agent with the IRS. On the other side was me, all by myself. That alone was very intimidating, which I'm sure was part of the plan.

They started out with some cordial conversation and then asked basic questions and verified my work history. They already had all the information, but it was just a way to build some rapport. It all seemed to be going smoothly, but they were clearly moving things forward for what they really wanted to talk about.

Things turned hot quickly after the warm-up. There is so much I don't remember about the interview; most of the questions they asked I don't remember. I do remember them asking me one question: "Is that your wife's signature on the 1003?" and I had to pause and think about the answer because all of this had happened three years prior to the interview. My mind was searching for the answer, and all of a sudden, one of them said, "We are keeping your wife out of this" (Tamela truly had no clue on anything and just signed paperwork if or when needed), "but you have one chance and one chance only to answer us correctly, and if you don't, then we will bring your wife in to be interviewed and consider pressing charges against her. You need to answer the question."

With this pressure applied, I finally remembered that day in the mortgage broker's office; the lender was asking for an updated 1003, and instead of taking it home to my wife, who had signed the original one, I figured I'd sign her name and it wasn't that big of a deal, because at the closing table she would have to sign the final 1003 anyway and it would be in the permanent records. It seemed harmless at that time, but they masterfully used that mistake to rattle me.

I was already willingly cooperating, but they had me dead to center with their well-timed and planned short outburst. I would do whatever was necessary to protect my wife, and they had done their homework and clearly knew that. We had been through so much already, and the last thing my wife needed was to be dragged into this nightmare.

At one point in the interview, I remember trying to pick up a glass of water they had set beside me, and my hand was shaking so badly from the intense pressure they were putting on me I had to put it back down quickly.

I left the nearly three-hour interview for a lonely drive home, my gut telling me this was not looking good—but holding out for a miracle. They were serious about filing charges. The mind is such a fascinating creation of God. We can "know" something is not looking good, but the ability of our mind to process reality can lag behind—which I believe is also a gift from God. They talk about the first stage of grief being denial. You might wonder how can that be, since there is clear evidence the person is gone. We know they are gone, and we talk about it, but the brain processing that reality and getting our emotions on the same page is a completely different process. I knew things did not go well that day driving home, but I was grasping for some ray of hope. Surely, we were going to be fine.

With my mind still in a fog from the intensity of that interview, I heard the dreaded sound of a flat tire. I thought, *Wonderful. Like it hasn't been a stressful enough day already.* I went to change the tire and realized I didn't have a lug wrench. I just wanted to get home, I just wanted to see my wife and explain to her about my day, and now this. *Lord, can nothing go right in my life anymore?* I ended up calling 911, and they sent roadside assistance to provide a lug wrench so I could get back on my journey home.

Several weeks later, I got the dreaded letter from a federal prosecutor explaining that I was going to be charged and listing the charges they were bringing up on me. The letter said if I couldn't afford a lawyer, one would be appointed. They were charging me with conspiracy, money laundering, and mortgage fraud. Reality hit. I closed my eyes many a night after losing our son and prayed that when I woke up in the morning the pain would just be gone. That deep ache in my heart was reappearing once again. I was getting a similar nauseous feeling that this wasn't going to go away, that my family was going be faced with yet another setback. Just when I thought life was back on track. *I guess life will never get back on track. I'm just doomed for constant failure.*

To fight the federal government, you need to have a bunch of money, and even then, the percentage of those who win a federal case is minimal. A federal charge is an entirely different beast.

I was given a court-appointed federal lawyer, and she began doing her due diligence on the matter. My attorney's investigator conducted several interviews with me by phone and helped review all the evidence. Then I was asked to come to Springfield to meet with my attorney personally.

Due to my wife's blood clot issues and long car rides being potentially very dangerous for her, she wasn't able to go with me on any of these trips. It was hard on her because she wanted to be there to support me. But it was close to nine hours of driving (round trip) and several hours of sitting in meetings all in one day; we just couldn't risk the potential health issues

I arrived at the attorney's office, and we had a lengthy conversation about the case. She then left me alone in the room to read the testimonies of what other people had said who were testifying against me. I sat there in absolute disbelief at some of the outright lies that were being told under oath. Anger began to swell up inside of me, and the more I read, the angrier I got. Finally, I had had enough, and I couldn't read it anymore. This was crazy.

It became clearer how I was being dragged into this. My attorney came back into the room. I said, "Surely the FBI knows that many of these statements are lies. All you had to do was talk to other people they mention to prove that." She said, "They most likely do, but this is what was said and recorded."

She told me that the other people in the marketing company had cut a deal to get a reduced sentence, which meant they had to bring something to the table, whether it was true or not. My attorney said that she had already asked about a deal for me, but since I was the last one in, I was at the bottom of the totem pole, and there was nothing more they needed.

I struggled with so much anger at first, but as time went on, I forgave them. I understood why everyone had acted the way they did. Everyone was simply looking out for themselves and their families and trying to cut deals. It doesn't make it right, but I could mentally grasp the motive of self-preservation. Over time, I began to pray for everyone involved, and prayed that everyone found God through this—and His favor!

During the meeting with my attorney, as she learned more about our history, she kept saying, "There is no way they should be considering jail time for you." She said, "Prison is genuinely supposed to be about reforming people, and you are already changed and being active in helping in the community and helping others—especially with your work at the counseling center."

She told me that a year ago, with my past and no previous criminal activity, this case was most likely an easy probation case, but with all the recent mortgage issues and the crashing mortgage market, the federal government was looking to make examples of people.

In the federal system, when you accept a plea deal, as part of that deal, you cannot argue for a lesser sentence. The judge may give you a lower or higher sentence from what is recommended, but you cannot make an argument for a lesser one.

With the evidence and testimonies (true or not), the others had all the odds in their favor. My attorney felt it was in my best interest to accept the plea deal. Part of me clearly wanted to fight the charges, and the other part of me just wanted this to be over with. Besides, the added threat that they would add more charges if I didn't go along with their plea was frightening. We also believed this was going to be a probation case, because I had never been in trouble before and had not even had a speeding ticket in my life. We would just take the probation and move on with life. *At least I won't be separated from my family.*

My lawyer said, "Based on what you are doing now, I'm going to ask the federal prosecutors to let us argue for a lesser sentence. But don't hold your breath because they are holding all the cards, and they rarely grant a request like this."

A week or so later, she called me. "You are not going to believe this," she said. "In all my years of practice, I've never had this happen before, but they are going to make a concession to the plea agreement and let us argue for a lesser sentence." Never underestimate the favor of God. That was a huge relief and restored confidence that God was opening the door for probation and no time served. Our spirits were lifted!

From the time I was first called in, things moved quickly. I was first interviewed in June, received the letter of the intent to charge me later that month, met with my attorney in July, and stood before a federal judge in September to officially plead guilty to the charges laid out in the agreement.

It is very intimidating to stand before a federal judge. I had never been in a courtroom before for something I had done. Yet, here I was, accepting my responsibility, agreeing to the plea deal, and pleading guilty to all charges. I drove home that day, and I just kept thinking, *I'm a felon; how did that happen? I'm a felon. I never dreamed I could even remotely be in this situation. I will no longer be known as Rick or a minister or a counselor. I will now forever be labeled as a felon. What an embarrassment, what a failure I am. I graduated from high school and college with such high hopes of a meaningful life, and here I am, facing this embarrassing and shameful failure.* These thoughts kept going round and round.

The Enemy is always trying to place labels on us. Labels that try to forever define who we are. "Felon" was one of those labels that, at that moment, I felt was going to be my legacy. The Enemy also tries to remind us how unworthy we are.

Once you plead guilty, you then meet with pretrial services. I was called back for yet another trip to Springfield to be interviewed by them and for them to start collecting information and building their sentencing worksheet. The worksheet is based on a point system to determine the recommended sentence. They look at the number of crimes, the dollar amount, whether you cooperated, whether you accepted responsibility, etc. There are positive and negative points for each item, and they come up with a score and a recommended sentence from that score.

I received my pretrial report in the mail a week later, and they were asking for thirty to thirty-six months. My heart sank. What happened to probation? Three years away from my family? This was another takotsubo moment. I felt another crushing blow to my already broken heart. *How much is one person supposed to take? Please, someone, wake me up from this nightmare.*

Going through trials often means there are days when we are on the mountaintop and full of hope and then days of crashing devastation. The longer the ups and downs from our struggles, the wearier and more hopeless we can become. I was weary from the process of bouncing from one high to the next low. I sensed there were darker days ahead; hope seemed to be galaxies away. I was trying to hold on to my faith, but harsh reality crush our faith if we aren't careful.

My sentencing hearing was set for February 11, 2010, my grandfather's birthday. Maybe that was a sign? That was a long time to be stuck in limbo. Between September and February was too much time to think about the bleak future, and I still had to get through all the dreaded holidays not only thinking about Landon being missing but now about the added fear of the future holidays *I* might be missing. Three years, three holidays away from my family. Our family table with two empty chairs.

My pastor walked with me each step of the way, and he took time out of his schedule to drive me down to Springfield for one of those trips. Once it was confirmed that I was going to have to accept the plea deal, he knew it was time to meet with the board and give full disclosure, since prior to this we weren't completely sure of what exactly would unfold.

I was not paid staff; I was basically an independent contractor who was using an office in the church for the counseling center. I clearly understood that whatever happened to me potentially impacted the church. I didn't really know any of the board that well. It was a large church with multiple services, and I had not crossed paths with most them. I spent an hour and a half giving full disclosure and walking them through the entire process.

Before I left, they were praying over me when one of the board members had a vision that he shared with everyone. He said he saw me being lifted out of a pit, and as I was being lifted out, there was still one animal clinging onto my leg. He said he felt the Lord showing him that I was close to being out of the pit and back on my way, but there was one last thing to be dealt with. It was a powerful moment and restored hope and encouragement to me at just the right time.

I left the boardroom and waited nervously for the call from my pastor to let me know what they had decided. He called and said, "The board is 100 percent behind you. Keep counseling and let God take care of things." In spite of our trials, we were so blessed to have people standing firmly behind us and recognizing the call of God on my life. The board was a huge blessing at this time!

February 11 came, the day of the sentencing. We had close to thirty people write letters to the judge on my behalf. Since we were allowed to argue for a lesser sentence, we were allowed to bring in a psychiatrist to talk about the trauma our family had already faced and how this additional trauma impacted the family. He specifically talked about my wife and, using some scoring chart that tracked trauma, said that she was near the top and that separation from her husband would have a major impact on the whole family. Then I had several other friends, including my pastor, stand before the judge and appeal for mercy at the sentencing.

My attorney stood before the judge and said that in all her years of practice, she had never met someone she was so sure should not go to prison as me.

The most brutal one to watch was my wife standing before the judge and trying not to cry as she pleaded our case, but her tears drowning out anything she was trying to say. My heart melted. How could I put my wife through this? *Why is this happening? She has suffered enough already.*

It's always hard to walk through dark trials, but it has always hurt me the most to see the brokenness of my family and the impact life has had on them.

My wife was politely but firmly cut off by the judge. From my perspective, it appeared his mind was already made up, and everything we had just presented and stated had little to no impact on him. He promptly started in on a firm lecture. This was at the crest of the mortgage crash. While I listened to him, fear and anxiety arose inside me. All I could think of was that this judge was extremely upset, and he was clearly looking for examples. I thought, *I'm not just going away for the recommended thirty to thirty-six months; he's getting ready to set a new standard and sentence me for life.*

There were approximately twenty-five friends and family who had made the long trip to be there in support of us during the hearing. It's hard to truly put into words what happened over the next few moments—but everyone in the courtroom witnessed it. The judge finished his stern lecture and raised his gavel to pronounce the sentence, and then he hesitated for just a slight moment. I have no doubt that it was the Holy Spirit whispering in his ear, changing his mind at the last possible moment, and when the gavel smashed down, he cut the sentence in half and gave me fifteen months.

I would have been devastated before the court hearing if I had known I was getting fifteen months. I had been completely convinced that with all the favor we had been shown and no past criminal history, I was going to be granted probation. But after hearing the judge's lecture and thinking I was going away for a long time, fifteen months sounded like a bargain.

My attorney felt that all the people who had showed up in support of me, sacrificing the long drive and missed time at work, had made a huge impact on the judge. I'm sure that definitely played a part, but I rest assured that God had orchestrated everything, and although it did not feel like it at that particular moment, God had answered prayers and was still in control.

There were probably forty-plus people who were involved in the marketing company or similar copycat groups that had started out on their own using a similar marketing/consulting agreement. Plus, there were multiple real estate agents involved in all the transactions, and yet, when it was all said and done, there were seven of us who were pulled out of the original group and charged. I never completely understood that. Still, in the end, I was given the lowest sentence, equivalent to one other person who had cut a deal and less than all the others who cut deals. God is the real deal worker!

I was waiting on the official letter. I knew I was going to report to a prison approximately four to five weeks after the sentencing. Hopefully, it was a prison camp, hopefully it was someplace warm, but there were no guarantees.

Our mentality changes once we grasp what is happening. This was real, I was going away, and I had about five weeks to prepare my family. I came back and started handing off my counseling clients to Frank, who was going to cover for me while I was gone. He was a trusted friend I'd met in school, while working on my bachelor's in Christian counseling.

I started the process of cleaning out my office one day. As I stood there with tears starting to form in my eyes, I flashed back to the first day when I opened the center—when all those emotions of gratefulness and excitement were flooding inside me for finally being where God wanted me. Hope was restored; I was dreaming again.

Now, I was cleaning out my office, and my emotions were at the opposite end of that spectrum. The joy and jubilation of opening the center were now replaced with despair and the all-too-familiar feeling of hopelessness. I felt my ministry was over. God could never use anyone like me now. I was a failure and forever a felon. I paused at the door and took one last glance as I walked out. When I closed that door, it felt like I had just closed the door to my dreams. *This is it.* It had been a great run, and I had been blessed to help many people in that office, but I'd never be back in ministry again. Now all I had to look forward to was a purposeless life.

The letter came about a week later, and I was told to self-surrender to Yankton Federal Prison Camp in South Dakota on March 22, 2010. After days of sulking and feeling the weight of depression with everything I was going to be missing—the birthdays, holidays, family dinners—my mind switched gears from sulking to how I could do something unique for my family, how I could let them know how much they meant to me. I started hatching a plan.

I went to Hallmark and purchased all the birthday/anniversary cards for the next year. I talked to my sister, and she agreed to mail them for me on the designated dates, and she was even kind enough to add a gift card for them. I handwrote a message in each card and mailed them all at once to her.

I decided to surprise my wife and planned a ceremony to renew our vows. I also decided to include my boys at the end of that ceremony. Of course, I've never been very good at keeping surprise secrets, but I knew I had to pull this off. Tamela deserved something special to boost us for what we were about to face.

I took my wife out for a nice lunch, and then we headed to a church with a small but beautiful wedding chapel that a friend had helped us secure. She had no idea what was going on; she was just asked to dress nice.

Pastor Joe had been a big part of our lives. He had married us, put us on staff as evangelist, dedicated our baby boys to the Lord, and preached our son, Landon's, funeral. He had been there with us through some of the best and worst times, and now he performed a beautiful and meaningful renewal ceremony for my wife and me. We had family and a few close friends attend.

At the end of the ceremony, the pastor called my two sons up to stand by us. He handed them each a dog tag that I'd made for them to wear while I was gone—a reminder of how proud I was of them—with a special note engraved specifically to each one. I also gave each of them a pocketknife. The pastor spoke to the family about the journey that lay ahead and prayed over us. It was a beautiful afternoon, cherishing my wife and boys.

Before I left for Yankton, I printed about twenty notes that said either "I love you" or "I miss you," and I hid them all over the house. At the bottom of the freezer, at the bottom of the clothes drawer, in kitchen cabinets, on plates, etc. Some of these were in the open and to be seen immediately, and others wouldn't be found until months later. But I wanted my family to know how special they were to me, and that although we had seen our share of heartache, we were going to somehow survive this also.

I was the last to leave the house that last day, so I slipped back into our bedroom to leave my wife a final note on her pillow, to find when she returned: "Tonight will be the loneliest night because it is the first night of a long year, but the good thing is, from here on out, each night alone brings us closer to being together again and forever."

All of us were paying a price. I just wanted my family to know how much I loved them and how proud I was of them.

CHAPTER 17

God Sent Jack

THE TIME HAD COME TO SELF-SURRENDER. Despair and hopelessness were my new best friends.

How many times does the Enemy threaten us with the maximum potential of our problem—the idea that whatever trial we are going through is a crushing blow? All we can see is all the negative of what we are going through. I had not even been to prison yet, but fear was gripping me at every level. The fear of the unknown at times seems worse than what is actually going on. Fear is always based on things that have not happened, and our imagination is masterful at taking a small obstacle and making a mountain out of it.

I don't fear the past; I fear the future. The same can be said about faith. I don't need faith to live my past; I need faith to make it through tomorrow, through my future. I need faith in God that will triumph over my fears.

I basically had two choices: *Do I surrender—or do I surrender?* Do I surrender to God's will and His plan and trust Him with my future, or do I surrender to fear and all life's problems and simply give up? Ultimately, during a trial, we will surrender to one or the other.

Now, we have reached, again, the moment the book began with. I had just walked into the control center and stated those words: "I'm Rick Unruh, and I'm here to self-surrender." The officer allowed me to say goodbye to my family before they left. The officer was kind enough to keep my family from seeing me being patted down and escorted away, so she waited for them to walk out of sight.

I was given an initial physical by a nurse and then given my badge that had to be on me at all times. Not having it on me would mean disciplinary action. I was given my prison khaki uniform and my bedding. I was instructed to walk up a hill to the dorm where all the new inmates initially stayed.

I weighed in at 318 pounds when they did my initial physical. I was out of shape and had to walk up a long hill, which could be challenging by itself, let alone while carrying my bedding and uniforms and some basic toiletries. The only things I was allowed to bring in with me were a Bible, my wedding ring, and my glasses.

Halfway up the hill, I was gasping for air, but when someone new is in camp, everyone stops what they are doing and just stands there and stares at you. Definitely awkward. Occasionally, I heard a wild remark about what is in store for the new prisoner. Between the anxiety and being out of shape for the uphill walk, I labored to gasp for each breath.

I had to keep moving. Occasionally I stopped to switch hands with what I was carrying, but in reality, I was just attempting to catch my breath. I finally made it to the dorm and checked in with the CO (commanding officer) on duty. He took me to the basement and showed me my bunk and locker. I was in a room with eighteen other inmates.

I made my bed and had my locker set up about the time everyone was being released from their work detail and heading back to their bunks for the 4 p.m. count. All the new prisoners are put together in the basement of the unit for about four to six weeks and then moved to other housing units.

After meeting the guys in my area and experiencing the first of many more counts to come, it was time for supper. Everyone took off, and I found myself frozen, trying to decide if I wanted to go eat or just skip it. Fear paralyzed me because I had no idea where I was supposed to sit. Everything I saw on TV talked about the gangs having certain areas in the cafeteria, and I was afraid if I sat in the wrong place, I could make enemies on day one.

Sometimes we are so focused on praying for deliverance *from* the fire that we miss seeing God's provision to make it *through* the fire. God's favor is always at work, even when we don't get the answer we were praying for; God is not going to abandon us, and even in prison, He had strategically placed people to assist me in my journey.

The first one God sent was Jack. Jack was in his 60s and had been in and out of prison most of his life. Despite living a hard life, he looked good and was more than willing to help the new guy. He started talking to me, gave me some helpful advice about some of the unwritten rules, and then asked me to join him for supper. Whew, what a huge relief. He would know where it was safe to sit. While he was walking with me to the chow hall, I asked him about how the seating works in Yankton. He chuckled and explained that we could sit wherever we wanted; this was a camp. I was so worried about something that wasn't even an issue. The Enemy is a master at causing worry over nothing.

Jack and I continued to visit over the next week, and then he was transferred out of our unit. I still, occasionally saw him on the walking track over the next year. But I'll never forget that, in the midst of my wilderness, God had planted Jack to help me settle into my new life.

God could have delivered me from prison, but I now understood that He knew this trial was going take me to levels of faith I never dreamed possible. He was going teach me to walk each day by faith, and at different critical times, He was going to send the right people to walk alongside me.

I love this saying that I heard on WAY-FM shortly after I was in prison: "Long before Zacchaeus couldn't see Jesus, a tree was already planted to meet his need." God sent Jack long before I entered Yankton, to bring me comfort.

It was time for our 10 p.m. count and my first night in prison. First of all, let me confess that I snore. I used to think I might be one of the worst snorers ever. But after bunking in a room with seventeen other guys, the sounds I heard all night long made mine seem mild. Some guys can rattle a bunk with their snoring.

I had finally settled into deep sleep when I was awakened by a flashlight in my eyes around 3 a.m. I sat straight up in bed, startled by the light, and wondering what was going on, only to realize it was the officer doing a mandatory count. They had to physically see your head, which meant shining the light directly on you. They do these counts at midnight, 3 a.m., and 5 a.m. You get used to them, and after the first few weeks, the light rarely woke me up.

There are red lights that light up to signify that count is under way, and that means that absolutely no leaving your bunk area until count is over. During one of those early counts, I woke up and had to go to the bathroom extremely badly. The bathroom was down the hallway. I started out the door, only to see that the red light was on and I had to wait. Is it just me or does time move extra slowly when you desperately have to go to the bathroom and you can't? It seemed like hours, waiting for count to clear. And, of course, on this particular night, there was a miscount, which meant they had to start all over again. It was beyond just having to go to the bathroom now; it was all-out pain, with water probably starting to fill up to my eyeballs.

Usually, you have your phone privileges set up within one to two days. But somehow mine had a glitch, and day after day, I went to the phone multiple times and typed in my code to see if it was working—and nothing. I so desperately wanted to call my family and just let them know I was okay because I knew they were worried about me, especially not being able to hear from me.

I kept checking with people who worked there, and they just said to be patient: "It will get turned on anytime now." I was able to borrow an envelope and stamp, and I sent out a letter to my family, letting them know that I was okay and would call as soon as I could. My letter reached them before I could actually use the phone.

One week after my arrival, after numerous daily complaints, my phone privileges were finally turned on, and I was able to start making calls. All phone numbers had to be preapproved, and we were given three hundred minutes per month, with a max of fifteen minutes at a time.

Needless to say, it didn't take long for those minutes to disappear, and trying to talk with my wife and each son was always a challenge in managing my allotted minutes.

I attended my first chapel service that Sunday, and God had a message that was spot-on for what I needed to hear. The chaplain referred to Ecclesiastes 7:8 as "the Romans 8:28 of the Old Testament." This Old Testament verse says, "Better is the end of a thing than its beginning, and the patient in spirit is better than the proud in spirit." The beginning leg of this journey had not been great, but God promised the end of matter was going to be better. All I was experiencing was going to work together and make sense in time, but it was going to take patience and perseverance. I was to trust Him and stay the course; the end was clearly going to be better.

The chaplain at Yankton played a huge role in my life, one that I will forever be grateful for. He invested so much time in me and basically began giving me equivalent-to-college-level courses on hermeneutics, the study and interpretation of the Bible. Those lessons are still ones I rely on today.

I said it earlier, and I will say it again: God could have completely delivered me from prison, but for whatever reasons, he allowed me to go through this wilderness experience. But he always had key people placed along the way to help me in my journey. He provided Jack to ease my fears, a chaplain who believed in me, a home church who stood with me, family members, and my former camp counselor who would be there for the season I am in currently in. God used this wilderness experience to prepare me for the promised land.

CHAPTER 18

The Power of Comfort

IF YOU WANT TO MEET BITTER PEOPLE, meet people who have been abandoned—by a parent, or by family, or by friends, at their greatest time of need. During my time in Yankton, I met hundreds of men battling bitterness—men who thought they had friends, but when things got tough, everyone seemed to disappear. You can imagine if someone is facing drug charges, friends aren't necessarily lining up to support them, because they don't want to be seen associating with someone who is being charged for drug-related issues and get drawn into their own legal problems.

In Psalm 38, we see the psalmist in a tough spot: his heart aches, his strength is failing, but more painful than that is that his friends are aloof. We see his hopelessness compounded by his loneliness. Loneliness is a multiplier of the hurt and pain we are experiencing.

> My heart throbs; my strength fails me,
> and the light of my eyes—it also has gone from me.
> My friends and companions stand aloof
> from my plague,
> and my nearest kin stand far off. (Psalm 38:10–11)

I witnessed multiple men receiving divorce papers while they were in prison. One inmate had moved his family to Yankton so his wife could be closer to him and be able to make every visit. Within a month, their relationship was already starting to deteriorate; eventually, she left Yankton to move back with her family and they ended in divorce, just another statistic. The stress and strain of the whole legal process is enough to potentially wreck any marriage. The investigation, the court dates, the waiting, the sentencing, the separation. It all can drive a wedge into marriages and families. Many times, especially the longer the sentence, the separation of prison is the final nail in the coffin.

But, in a lot of ways, prison is tougher on the families left behind than on the prisoners themselves. Follow me on this: prisoners are burdened, suffering from a loss of freedom and missing their families, and, yes, they feel the pain of what they have lost. But after a time of adjusting, our minds begin to shift, and we learn to stay focused on surviving in our own little community. We don't have the daily pressure of provision. We don't worry about what we are going to eat or how we are going to pay rent or utilities. We are locked into our own culture with our own set of routines.

I saw many families trying to survive in horrible circumstances, when the primary breadwinner or a significant contributor to the monthly budget was now gone. For the most part, the bills didn't change. The rent was still the same, as were the insurance and vehicle payments; the kids were still hungry—and if there were teenage boys, you know what that does to a food budget. Then there was the embarrassment that the kids faced when people asked them where their dad was and why he wasn't around anymore. Kids would no longer have a little extra money to be able to go to the movies or to go grab some ice cream with friends. Life changes drastically for families, and survival becomes a daily battle. In the midst of trying to survive and not being able to see each other, many couples begin to drift.

In 2 Corinthians 11, we see Paul being open and honest, sharing that he is worn down and exhausted. We can easily understand the outward affliction—everywhere he went, there were the dangers of just basic traveling in that day, and then there were those trying to stop his ministry, even resorting to physical attacks. In verses 24 to 28, he shares the dangers and the troubles he has faced but ends with the daily pressure he feels for the churches:

> Five times I received at the hands of the Jews the forty lashes less one. Three times I was beaten with rods. Once I was stoned. Three times I was shipwrecked; a night and a day I was adrift at sea; on frequent journeys, in danger from rivers, danger from robbers, danger from my own people, danger from Gentiles, danger in the city, danger in the wilderness, danger at sea, danger from false brothers; in toil and hardship, through many a sleepless night, in hunger and thirst, often without food, in cold and exposure. And, apart from other things, there is the daily pressure on me of my anxiety for all the churches.

The internal fears seem a little harder to comprehend because Paul was such an amazing man of faith. Was his faith at risk? I don't believe that for one minute. Was he tired? Yes, he was human. In another part of this letter, he writes, "Our bodies had no rest" (2 Corinthians 7:5). When we don't get enough rest, and we are constantly on the move, mistreated, and physically drained, it has a direct impact on our emotions. We know from Paul, he was carrying the heavy burden of the churches he had ministered to, and he had recently written a firm letter to the Corinthians, rebuking them for believing false teaching.

People in ministry can face a similar feeling. Carrying the weight of your congregation is tiresome at times. Sometimes it feels like you are simply running from one crisis to another, and victories seem to be few and far between during different seasons. Of course, it isn't that victories are truly few and far between, but when members typically make an appointment to see their pastor, it usually involves a major life decision or a severe problem they are facing. So many times, pastors are bombarded with tough issues, and the burden of seeing what people are facing wears on us.

It's interesting how Paul states this in 11:28—"and, apart from other things"—implying that he could have kept going with his list of things that had happened to him. But, on top of everything, he comes back to his anxiety, or his intense concern, for the church. This is the same intense concern that pastors feel for their flocks when people are hurting.

The remedy for life's problems can be quite simple in many situations. It's precisely what Paul discovered with the visit from Titus: All comfort ultimately comes from God (2 Corinthians 1:3). We often picture the comfort of God as an angel coming down and putting us under their wings while we recover—and I have no doubt that God does that at times, but more often than not, God chooses to use people to be dispensers of His comfort.

Paul writes, "For even when we came into Macedonia, our bodies had no rest, but we were afflicted at every turn—fighting without and fear within. But God, who comforts the downcast, comforted us by the coming of Titus, and not only by his coming but also by the comfort with which he was comforted by you, as he told us of your longing, your mourning, your zeal for me, so that I rejoiced still more" (2 Corinthians 7:5–7).

This is Paul, who had had some amazing supernatural experiences, from the Damascus road to visiting the third heaven. God could have given him another visit to heaven or sent an angel down to comfort him, but God chose to use Titus. "But God, who comforts the downcast, comforted us by the coming of Titus" (v. 6). Paul's comfort clearly came from God but was dispensed by Titus's coming to him in a time of need.

Never underestimate the power of God to use you to bring comfort to others. A timely phone call, a letter in the mail, an invite to have lunch—you never know how these small actions may change someone's life at a pivotal point. We have to look beyond the surface smiles on people's faces and pray for discernment to be used to bring comfort to hurting people.

Sometimes, the church has simplified comfort to simply mean, "Come down to the altar, and we will pray for you, and you will experience God's comfort." That is a super important step, and I am not minimizing the importance of it at all. But comfort doesn't end there. The Greek word for "comfort" carries the meaning of walking alongside someone. Are we willing to walk alongside hurting people—to seek them out during the week, outside of church, and encourage them?

We do experience comfort at the altar many times, but then we have to go back and face life—possibly even a horrible situation. Many times alone, we feel overwhelmed. Walking alone through a trial of life is not the way God designed the body of Christ to function. But, rather, we carry one another's burdens; we walk alongside those who are hurting.

Many well-meaning Christians come up with clichés to attempt to bring us comfort. But what we long for is someone to walk alongside us and cry with us. Just being there in those moments says more about our friend's faith and love for us than any words can at that moment.

Comfort is contagious. When you read the next verse of 2 Corinthians 7, you see how contagious it can be. The church comforted Titus, and then Titus comforted Paul. It started with a church body comforting Titus, which led to the church playing a huge part in Paul's comfort through the comfort they gave Titus. Their repentance after Paul's previous letter encouraged Titus and eventually soothed Paul's intense concern for the church. We are all potential dispensers of God's comfort. All of us have a calling to be stewards of this gift.

We often think of the word "steward" as simply referring to money, but a steward is one who manages the possessions of another. If we have experienced God's comfort and we are in possession of it, then we are obligated to manage it—and that does not mean to just bury it. Rather, are we using God's comfort the way He intended it—to help other people struggling in life?

I witnessed this life-changing comfort firsthand while I was in Yankton. There were dark days in the beginning, and I felt like I was in a daze most of the time. The purpose in life I had recently found with the Dream Again ministry was now lost. My mind was dominated with self-accusatory, negative thoughts. Yankton prison may have just been for eleven and a half months, but the imprisonment of failure and lack of purpose felt more like a life sentence.

One of the first letters I sent out was to my dad. I was so full of shame, and the embarrassment of going to prison seemed like too much. My dad had worked so hard, had become a respected businessman in the community, and was known as a dedicated Christian. I had severely failed both my father and my mother, and the thought of this haunted me, rattling me to the very core of who I was. In the height of my shame, I sent my dad this note:

> Dad, I have brought such shame and embarrassment to our family. Why don't you just disown me and change my last name and take me out of the will. I don't even deserve to be called an Unruh. I'm sorry that I am such a failure.

I felt like I was drowning in a sea of regret. Those early

days in prison, my mind was constantly replaying my list of failures, strengthening the grip regret now held on my life, as it tried to strangle the little hope I once had.

My sister Krista was a godsend. She rallied the troops to make sure everyone was staying engaged and encouraging me, as well as my family. She started a private Facebook group, inviting many friends and urging them to make sure they were writing to me. If they wanted to post me a note on the Facebook page, she printed them out once a week and mailed them to me.

For the first thirty days, I received five to fourteen letters every day. One day, I was standing by Clarence, a fellow inmate, for mail call. My name had just been called multiple times, Clarence leaned over and said, "I don't know why they call this 'mail call'; they should just call it 'Unruh call,' because you are the one getting all the mail."

Those letters were a lifeline. I imagine most people had no idea of what a difference a few sentences on a card meant to me, and how this encouragement began to shift the tide that was trying to drown me. Each day, I grabbed my mail, headed back to my bunk, and slipped it under my pillow. I waited for everyone to leave for supper, because I knew that most likely I was going to be crying while I read those letters. My bunk was in the back corner, and when everyone was finally gone, I opened my mail, and naturally, the tears began to flow. The longing to be with my family and the loss of all the things I was missing at home hit with harsh and depressing reality.

But day after day, I was getting strong words of encouragement, words of comfort from my family and friends. They kept saying, "Rick we believe in you, don't quit, God still has a plan." And although I severely doubted that God still had a plan for me, the more I read those letters day after day, it started to turn my heart, and I started to allow myself to think, *Maybe, just maybe, God can still use me.*

The maybes turned into *Yes, He can still use me*, and a renewed faith arose inside of me. It started with people who were willing to walk alongside me, to bring comfort to me, to speak into my life. I began to realize I wasn't walking alone, that people still believed in God's call on my life. In the midst of my tears of pain, there were also tears of joy from the hope that people were imparting to me. *Maybe, just maybe.*

I missed Darian's junior year of baseball and most of his senior year also. One day I received a note from him that made me very proud, yet it was also a painful reminder of the time I could never reclaim. I had missed him hitting the first home run of his high school baseball career. He wrote,

> I miss you a lot, Dad. Baseball just isn't the same without you sitting in the stands, and watching how much you enjoy watching the game. This coming-up year will be a long one, but it is pushing me to be better. I can't wait till I can give you my home run ball and just give you a big hug. I wear the necklace you gave me under my shirt every game and practice to remind me that you may be in South Dakota, but you are always near my heart. I hope that you are doing okay I can't wait to see you.
>
> Love,
> Your youngest son

Here are some other words from friends that were lifting me up during this time. Randy and Denita Smith wrote:

> Rick, been thinking of you and your family today. I know it had to be a tough day. Randy and I are here for Tamela, Darian, and Dake. You know that they can always call us for anything. I am going to give Tamela

a call this week; maybe we can have a girls night! We
love you guys!

From Melissa Cox:

Hey Rick! Mom, Dad, and I are praying for you and
your family! You have all of our LOVE and SUPPORT!
God is going to do INCREDIBLE things through all of
this! Wow! What a TESTIMONY you will have! Love
you all so much!

From Cheri Unruh Stancer:

My heart is heavy this morning. It is day 4, and I
know reality has sunk in. My prayers are for you and
the family. May God keep your mind sound and your
spirit encouraged. This is a "bump" in the road to the
rest of your life. We are here for you to support you
and love you and help you get to the next level that
God has for you.

Love you so much,
Cheri

Delnita Hazel wrote:

Rick, been thinking about you a lot the past couple of
days. Miss your presence around the building here. Miss
harassing ya...haha. Miss chatting with you. However, I
know that God is continuing to work a miracle in your
life through this situation. Just want ya to know I'm
thinking about you!

Alan McCamey wrote:

> Hi Rick. I have found that I think of you most every day and hope/trust that you are steadily plodding your way through this. I am proud of you, as well as your family, for dealing with this unfortunate situation with strength and integrity. It has warmed my heart to read your son's posts on here to you. This ordeal is awful, but it will give him an appreciation for what really matters in life, just as our situation has made men out of my boys and taught them things that I probably never would have been able to teach them. I'm glad you and I connected online shortly before you had to report. That was great. Hang in there, bud.

There is nothing more devastating than being in a battle and being forgotten by those closest to you. But there is nothing more encouraging and motivating than to be surrounded by friends who still believe in you, even at your lowest point. I believe carrying one another's burdens and walking alongside each other is one of our greatest calls to ministry in the church. The power of comforting one another is a life changer! I know; it changed my life.

Those letters and words of comfort and encouragement carried me through some long, confusing days. And with time, I even started to find humor once again, like the day my son, Dake, called. He was moving to Kansas City and super excited about a new job opportunity. He started telling me about his new apartment and how nice it was, and then he said, "It's even gated! So I can tell people that I actually live in a gated community."

I chuckled and replied, "Son, I also live in a gated community, and I can tell you firsthand, it's not all it's cracked up to be!"

CHAPTER 19

45 Hamburgers to Go

E VEN BEFORE OUR FIRST VISIT, heartache hit on the home front. My wife already had her hands full with keeping the household in order and dealing with the emotions of missing her husband. Then her uncle lost his battle with cancer. After attending your son's funeral, any funeral stirs fresh memories of that day, and the added burden that I was not be able to be by her side to support her was so difficult on both of us.

Then, Coco, the poodle we'd had since before Landon passed, died shortly after I went into Yankton. Landon loved Coco, and when he came in from playing outside, he would sit on the couch and let Coco start licking his sweat off his legs. My wife and I never understood how he let Coco do that, but he loved that dog. It was more than just losing a family dog; it was losing another piece of Landon's life we all shared.

I initially went into prison counting the days until I was released. But those were such big numbers, and it seemed like it was forever. Eleven and half months is not a real long time. But in a tough situation, it still feels like forever.

Every Wednesday at Yankton was hamburger day. I actually preferred to call it "condiment day" because I love condiments and mixing multiple sauces together when I eat. But in Yankton, all you had was salt and pepper. Except on Wednesdays, when there was a full bar of condiments:

ketchup, mustard, onion, mayo, pickles, lettuce, tomato. And we could get as much as we wanted. Some days I think I had more of a condiment burger with a hamburger patty thrown in there somewhere!

I came to the conclusion that I no longer wanted to count how many days I had left, but rather, how many hamburgers I had left to eat. Instead of 315 days, I started my first hamburger countdown with only forty-five more burgers to eat before I was released! It's interesting how changing the way we think about something can impact our mood and entire thought process, our perspective. I thought to myself, *I have no problem eating 45 hamburgers!*

I made it my goal to use this time to *grow* spiritually and *shrink* physically! I accomplished both of those goals.

There was a walking track, and when I first reported, making it around the track once was about all I could handle. I started walking it once after breakfast, lunch, and dinner, while I built up my stamina.

We were allowed to have earphones and a Walkman radio. To have a portable Walkman cassette player or eventually a Walkman CD player when I was in high school and college was a big deal. I traveled to many a basketball game listening to it on the team bus. But honestly, until prison I had no idea the brand was still around. I put my earphones in, tuned it to K-LOVE, a Christian music station, and started walking the track while praying and meditating. My absolute favorite moments were when the Newsboys song "I Am Free" was played. I cranked up the volume and wanted to just take off running, imagining the day I would be free! I would think of what I would do when I first heard that song in church after my release! It's so easy to lose value in your freedom, until it is totally taken away. I now had a new appreciation and a reason to celebrate freedom.

On many occasions, a friend joined me on the track, and instead of listening to my Walkman, my walk quickly became a social or witnessing/counseling time. Little did I know that my quest to get into better shape also would also become an excellent opportunity to witness to people.

Alone time is nearly impossible to find in prison, so I cherished the walks, especially in the dark when not very many people were out. I do not like the cold! I often wondered why God couldn't have sent me to Florida for prison. I'm much more suited for Florida! Even on warmer days, I can have a difficult time keeping my hands and feet warm. But I longed for some form of private time. So I spent many a winter's night in South Dakota walking the track in the bitter cold, and even in below-zero weather, I was out. I layered every piece of clothing I could find, put on the heavy coat they provided, wrapped a scarf over my face, put a hat on my head and my heavy work boots on my feet, and went out to walk. This was something I never imagined doing at home, because I would be inside my warm house. But it was a priceless time for me to refocus, pray, and think about my future. Many nights I was so lost in worship and prayer that I didn't even think about the cold.

With 43 hamburgers left, I experienced my first shakedown. I had just moved over to my new housing unit when an officer walked in and told us we needed to leave: "This is a shakedown." *Shakedown? What's that?* The officers proceeded to block off our cube, which was made up of two rows of four bunks on each side and lockers in between the bunks. The officers then started digging through everyone's locker, looking for contraband (anything illegal, from tobacco to an unauthorized magazine). Even though they had every right to look through all our stuff and I had nothing to hide, it was still an awkward feeling. All you own in prison fits into that one locker. Everything else around you is shared property. Your locker is the only privacy; it's the only space that is just yours. And there they are, digging through it. Just like people who have had their house burglarized, you feel violated in some way because your privacy has been invaded, and someone has looked through your personal items.

The biggest shakedown I experienced in Yankton happened when I had about eight hamburgers left to eat. An officer had discovered the mother lode of all contraband. We were all escorted into small rooms for well over an hour, probably closer to two, and of course I needed to use the restroom, and there was no way they were letting us out of that room while they were in the middle of a major shakedown of the entire dorm.

They found plenty of contraband, but nothing that led them to the mother lode. So, they took our microwaves, and some other privileges were taken away from us until someone confessed. Having microwaves taken was a big deal. About ten days passed, there were still no answers, and the men were getting a little cranky. The warden finally gave us back our microwaves and privileges, and to the best of my knowledge, they never found out who had hidden the contraband.

But this first time, I watched from the hallway and thought to myself, *What if God were to call a shakedown right now? If God were to stop by and openly dig through our secret thoughts and actions right now. If Christ were to walk in and take inventory of our life, would He say, "Well done, good and faithful servant"? Or would we want to run for cover from the embarrassing things we know He would find?* We know that Christ sees our hearts, but we often think things done in secret will not be known by anyone. Yet there is the ultimate shakedown that is coming when we will all stand before God and give account.

God's shakedown is not concerned with the outside or how things appear, but with what is in our hearts, what we have stuffed in our locker. I challenge you to take a few moments and evaluate where you are with God and what is in your heart. Make this your prayer:

Search me, O God, and know my heart! [Shake down my heart!]

> Try me and know my thoughts!
> And see if there be any grievous way in me,
> and lead me in the way everlasting! (Psalm 139:23–24)

CHAPTER 20

Feels like Christmas Morning

VISITATION WAS ONLY ALLOWED once every three weekends. The hours were 5–9 p.m. Friday, 10 a.m.–4 p.m. Saturday, and 9 a.m.–2 p.m. Sunday. If your weekend happened to fall on a holiday, you received an extra day on Monday.

The only time my wife wasn't able to come was the very first time, because of my son's high school prom; we both knew she needed to stay there for that and support Darian. But waiting six weeks to see my family was an added difficulty.

The night before each visit, I felt like a kid on the night before Christmas. Sleep was elusive, with the anticipation of seeing my wife and boys. On Friday, we finished our 4 p.m. count, and then I got dressed in my khakis, even ironing them for this big occasion. Weather permitting, I always waited outside, near the visiting room, pacing around in anticipation of hearing my name called over the intercom. My wife always got there early and stood in line to be one of the first ten names called.

When I heard my name, excitement burst inside of me, and I took off running. Every time I entered the visiting room, my heart was pounding to see the most beautiful woman I knew and the greatest gift God had given me—my family. Tamela had to make so many sacrifices to keep the family functioning during this year, and then add a painful six-hour drive, especially with her history of blood clots, causing her to need to stop and walk around every few hours. She had to spend two nights in a motel, three days in a visiting room, and then the lonely trek back home to reminisce on our time together, knowing she'd be going home to an empty bed once again. She is, indeed, one of a kind.

The visiting room was simple: a large, open room with chairs lined up in rows facing each other. In the summer, there were round tables outside that we could sit at during visitation. There were typically eighty to one hundred people in there (counting inmates and visitors). Visitors couldn't bring anything in with them, except for money in a clear bag for the vending machines. Never in my wildest dreams did I ever think I would look forward to eating from a vending machine, but it was a royal treat. Probably because I was sharing it with family and friends! Everything tastes better when you are with your family.

People sometimes ask, "What did you talk about for all those hours?" Because our relationship was built on two years of long-distance dating and letter writing, we had developed a deep level of communication; there was never a shortage of what to say, and my wife kept me updated on what was happening on the home front. The visitation weekends always went by too fast.

Then it was time to say goodbye. Where had the time gone? Talk about two extreme emotions! The excitement and anticipation to see my wife became covered by a cloud of heartbreak as I said farewell again. Even as my name was called on Sundays to come to the visiting room, the reality was already setting in, and I was much more somber, not wanting the last day to end. It had to be harder for Tamela; my wife finished our visit, and she still had a six-hour trip home that night, after an emotional weekend. I went back to my bunk and just lay there in a numb state. *Let the countdown begin: only three more hamburgers until*

I get to see my family again. After each visit, it seemed like the next two to three days dragged interminably.

After one visit, I went back to my bunk and penned this letter to my wife:

> Dear Tamela, it's always such a sad day to see you go. I tried hard today not to let myself get depressed before you and the boys left. But I clearly failed. Fridays are like being on a mountaintop in anticipation to see you and then a crashing valley when it comes time to telling you goodbye. It never gets easier; instead, it feels like it gets harder each time. I long to be with you every day. And yet with each sorrowful goodbye, we are that much closer to being back together again. I am such a blessed man to have a woman like you to share my life with.

My sons, other family members, and friends also made the drive to show their support. It was humbling to see the sacrifices they made.

Here are a few comments from letters written to the Facebook group from family and friends who had visited me; Krista had posted these on the private Facebook page.

Randy and Denita wrote:

> All joking aside, we were so glad that we could visit Rick. We need to keep him and his family in our prayers; the camp that he is in is probably the most beautiful camp in the entire prison system. As Tamela has mentioned, it is an old college campus, and the yard and flowers are neatly groomed. I know that we all wanted him closer, but after seeing the place, we realized that God knew what he was doing! We can't wait to visit him again.

My cousin Laurie, who made it part of the family vacation to stop by and spend a few days with me, said:

> This past weekend I was able to go to South Dakota
> with my family. We had a great time with Rick and
> Tamela, Dake and Darian. I'm not sure if we could have
> been in a more beautiful place to visit. The grounds of
> the prison were gorgeous. Flowers and beautiful shade
> trees to sit under while we visited were everywhere.
> It was funny to see Rick answer all of my son Trey's
> questions. Funny ones like "Why can't we go run on
> that track?" to "Are you in a cell?" We had some good
> laughs, and Rick was so patient with him. Trey even
> made this paper airplane to fly, and when he flew it, let's
> just say it went "out of bounds."
>
> The biggest thing I took from this memorable week-
> end is the foundation of Christ we hold as a family.
> Many of you have known Rick for many years. You
> have seen the good moments, the tragic moments, and
> now the moments of waiting. Pray for him and Tamela
> that they will stand firm during this time of waiting.
> Pray that they would have an extra measure of guid-
> ance and endurance to lead them through their times of
> separation. Pray that Rick's witness at this prison camp
> will lead others to become active in the faith. I came
> away from the weekend knowing that in the midst of
> this situation we have a God who loves us. He cared
> enough about Rick to place him in the perfect prison
> that defies all of what any of us could imagine a prison
> looks like. Our foundation is definitely built on The
> Solid Rock!

Krista:

Rick was telling me about all the meals he has learned
to cook in the microwave, and I know you're thinking
to yourself—big deal?!—but the amazing part is how
these guys come up with things like pizza, quesadillas,
Thai noodles, or even desserts like cakes, all out of the
small ingredients they are allowed to buy once a week.
For those of you who know me well and know that our
family owned a restaurant growing up, you know that
I do not like cooking and try to avoid it at all costs. I
have asked Rick for his microwave recipes, as my meals
could use some sprucing up; he laughs, but I'm serious.

I wish that I could make it out there more often—it
was so great seeing Rick (again—being forced to say
nice things about my brother is hard)—and for those
of you who plan to go or are thinking about going, it
really is a nice little town and a great time with Rick.

7 more months; according to Rick, just twenty-eight
more hamburgers...

I honestly cannot say this enough, and I know that
Tamela and our whole family agrees: we can't thank
you all enough for the love, support, and prayers! Now
I have to get back to pestering Rick before he starts to
whine.

Krista

From my wife:

The first question I asked him on our first visit: Was he
really all right, and is he really being treated okay? Rick
assured me he is doing fine.

Rick told me he is nice to everyone and minds his
own business, he has learned areas to avoid that may

cause potential issues, he is keeping busy working on his master's degree and writing to all of us back home and taking naps when there is nothing else to do. I think he should be all caught up by the time he gets home, so there will be no more napping for him. Lol.

I updated him about how Dake's new job is going, since he's not able to be there with us on this trip. Darian had a lot of catching up to do with Rick, filling him in on how his baseball season was going, how prom went, and how he did on his ACT, and lots of other father/son talk. I watched as Darian and Rick talked, and I could see how both their eyes lit up as they enjoyed the time they were able to spend together.

The visits were never long enough, but they gave me something to look forward to. It's sad to realize that quite a few men never received any visits while they were at Yankton. I was blessed with great family and friends and God's provision to allow them to come to visit.

CHAPTER 21

Work Diet

PRISON IS ALL ABOUT ROUTINES and boundaries. Since this was a camp, there were no tall fences at Yankton. There was only a short, decorative fence that went around the camp. Some have said, "No fences? What stopped inmates from escaping?" These were all low-risk inmates to begin with, and many of them had been in a higher security prison and had earned the right to move to a less restrictive camp. Zero tolerance—being shipped to a higher security prison, with more time added to your sentence if you crossed a boundary—was a very clear yet invisible fence that kept anyone from walking off. The consequences were too high.

Yankton Federal Prison Camp was actually right in the middle of town, surrounded by houses on all sides. The high school football field was directly across the street, and on Friday nights in the fall, we saw the lights and heard the roar of the crowd. This brought back great memories of the many nights I went to games as a child and or took my wife and boys. This also caused reflection on the night I got the worst phone call of my life.

At the prison, everyone was assigned a job. After several days of being there, I was assigned to the maintenance department (if you knew me, you'd know how hilarious it was that they were relying on me to keep the place maintained).

With over nine hundred inmates, there was no way to keep all of them busy. Out of the fifty guys that were assigned to that particular maintenance group, ten to fifteen guys actually did the work. Most of them had expertise in that area. The rest of us had no choice but to sit in a room on benches that had been slapped together with plywood. Those were terribly long days, and time seemed to pass at a snail's pace.

One day, a Christian brother found me and informed me that they had an opening where he worked, and I should apply. The job was repairing tape recorders for the blind for the Library of Congress. I had no clue what that would be like, but anything was better than sitting on that hard bench all day. I applied and was accepted for the position. The favor of God at work again!

We were all seated at a large conference table, and each of us had a comfortable office chair to sit in a while working. The tools we used were carefully accounted for each morning and at the end of the shift before they were locked up. The busyness and chatter of the day helped keep time moving.

It was here that I heard a new term that made me laugh: "work diet." We had two groups. The cleaners and the repairmen. The cleaners cleaned the cases for the recorders and prepared each machine for the repairmen. If the exterior case was broken or cracked, they replaced the casing. Once that was completed, they sent them on to the repair area. On this particular day, we were told that the previous week we'd had a near record week and sent out over one hundred refurbished/repaired tape players. Normally, we were at around sixty-five to seventy-five a week. This volume threw the cleaners into a panic because they saw that their stash was depleted, and they needed to work extra hard to catch up. One of the cleaners stood up and informed us that this week the repairmen were going to be put on a "work diet"!

We need to cut our production a little, because too much productivity threw them all out of their normal routine of how many machines they had to get cleaned in a day. The work diet worked great in prison, but I'm afraid it isn't well suited for the real world.

Most of the men in the room were very cynical toward Christianity, and several were dedicated members of the Asatru religion, which I had never heard of before. Asatru is ancient Norse paganism. They were very loyal to their pagan religion, and I listened to them, day after day, talking about their numerous gods. Any mention of Christianity evoked some harsh and passionate responses.

After months of being locked in that room with them every day, I had no issues with the men that I worked with; it was just the topics they discussed all day, the negativity, and the constant bantering about Christianity that was wearing on me.

In late April, I was moved from the basement to my new dorm. I was devastated. I had just settled into a routine and was forming some good friendships with those in my other dorm. I had connected with some great Christian brothers who gathered in the lobby each night. They boldly stood there in a circle, holding hands and praying. Once I was moved to another dorm, it was out of bounds to enter my previous dorm, and my new home did not have a group of guys who were praying together.

I was starting all over again. But God is always in control, even when it feels like He isn't. I was placed in a cubicle area with sixteen guys, and for the most part, everyone got along. It's the small things God does for us; we see His favor. For example, I was used to sleeping with a small fan attached to the bottom of the bunk above me and blowing on my face. It was more about hearing the noise than anything else. The way those cubicles were set up, only about six guys had access to an outlet for the fan. With God's favor, my bunk assignment was one that had an outlet for my fan. Just a small reminder that God was with me.

Being a heavy sleeper was a necessity for that area. The head of my bunk was directly against the block wall that separated our living area from the computer/game room. Guys stayed up late playing cards on the weekends. But they weren't exactly quiet, and the game tables were plastic. Each time they slammed a card down, it created a loud noise. If the other guy had a better hand, then he had to hit the table harder, so he wasn't disrespected. It was extremely noisy once those games got started.

Another Christian brother told me about a night orderly position that came open. This allowed me more flexibility to work on my master's degree during the day and allow for more opportunities for quiet and uninterrupted study time. He was also working on some classwork to get his license for ministry when he was released. He had been a very successful businessman who had been caught up in some tax issues and was sentenced to three years in prison.

This Christian brother had been very successful in the sales world and that eventually led him to be able to own his own companies. Now, he would joke with me about the tough decision he was facing in choosing what "restaurant" he was going to eat at that particular night. Prison becomes its own interesting community, with people showing their entrepreneurial skills. There were "stores" for getting things fixed, for purchasing food items, and for artists to hand-draft you a personalized card to send home. There were also restaurants. My friend had a list of different guys who could prepare delicious meals from a microwave. I know it sounds bizarre, but they actually tasted pretty good, and the guys were quite creative in how they fixed the meals. The Christian man rotated from Mexican, to Italian, to Chinese, pizza, or Korean, to some specialty American dishes. One of the moistest cakes I have ever had in my life came from a prison microwave and used the secret ingredient of a Coke.

Becoming a night orderly also meant a significant pay raise. I was going from seventeen cents an hour to twenty-nine cents an hour! I was rolling in the dough!

My specific job as a night orderly was to clean the control center—the central command of the prison. This was the same spot where I'd first checked in, the same place I'd uttered those prophetic words: "I'm Rick Unruh, and I am here to self-surrender."

Once a week, I had to go clean the segregated housing unit (SHU). This was made up of three cells, with maximum security protocols. Each cell had two bunks, a small desk on each side, a shower, and a toilet—and about five feet of a walkway between beds. It was super congested when four people were locked up at once. The SHU was used as a punishment for a few weeks for breaking the rules or bad behavior, or it was a holding cell for those being shipped out to a higher security prison for some infraction.

Major discipline issues were rare because there was a zero-tolerance policy. If you were caught doing something illegal or fighting, then you were shipped to a higher security prison. For the most part, the camp was quiet, but when you have hundreds of men living in a confined area, conflict is sure to arise at times.

I witnessed two specific fights. One started on the basketball court. I was on the top level riding a stationary bike when it broke out. Inmates got in the middle of it to break it up, and it appeared that it was over, and nothing more than a brief scuffle had ensued. But a few moments later, I saw someone chasing after another man carrying a folding chair over his head to hit the other inmate. Once again, it was quickly broken up by the inmates. Everyone left the gym, and I figured that was the end of it. But once they were outside in the yard, it quickly escalated again. Now about fifteen guys were involved in a small brawl out in the public areas. Due to zero tolerance, all of them were shipped out ASAP.

The other fight happened in the dorm. It was a brief scuffle that had been building for some time. It finally escalated to a few shoves. I was told that one of the guys, who was a few cubicles over and a pretty quiet guy, calmly walked back to his bed and started putting on his steel-toed work boots. He said, "If I'm going to get shipped"—because someone is likely to tell, and no matter who started it, both get shipped—"I'm going to at least make it count." He gave away some items from his locker to a few friends, knowing he would not be back, then he left to chase down the other inmate, and a bloody fight broke out before the officers could get it stopped. They were both escorted out to the SHU and shipped out quickly.

For me, this was my typical day, once I became a night orderly:

> 5:30 a.m.—Wake up and go to the study room to do my morning Bible study.
>
> 8:00 a.m.—Back to bunk for the count (those who had day jobs are counted at work).
>
> 8:30 a.m.—Count clears.
>
> 9:00–11:00 a.m.—Do classwork or read a book if no classwork during this time.
>
> 11:00 a.m.—12:00 p.m.– Lunch.
>
> 12:15 p.m.—Count, back at my bunk.
>
> 12:45 p.m.—Count clears.
>
> 1:00–2:30 p.m.—Go to the gym to exercise or walk outside.
>
> 2:30–4:00 p.m.—Take a shower and then usually take

a nap (Truthfully, anytime you could take a nap, you took advantage of it, because it always made time go quicker.)

4:00 p.m.—Standing count at your bunk for everyone.

4:30–5:30 p.m.– Supper.

5:30–10:00 p.m.—Work.

10:00 p.m.—Count at bunk and lights out.

12 a.m., 3 a.m., and 5 a.m.—The officers do a count throughout the night while we are sleeping.

CHAPTER 22

Roses—in Prison?

T HERE WAS THE FREEDOM TO MOVE about the prison campus, but you always had to sign in or out at your dorm and let them know exactly where you were going. Every so often, a lockdown census was called to verify that information, and if you weren't where you were supposed to be, then you were going to face disciplinary action.

I remember one particular lockdown census. You could almost call it a game of freeze tag. When you heard "lockdown census" over the intercoms, you immediately froze, wherever you were. Officers locked the buildings and watched the exits so no one could come or go while they verified everyone was where they should be. The purpose was simple: if you weren't where you were supposed to be, then you were out of bounds and faced the disciplinary board and most likely received a "shot"—the slang term for any behavior infraction.

A shot usually involved some extra work duty for first-time offenders, and then it moved to losing privileges, such as gym privileges.

One time, I was near my rack (the inmate term for a bunk or bed) around 1:30 p.m., when I heard "lockdown census" come across the intercom. Next thing I heard was a guy shouting "Oh, (bleep)!" as he frantically started running down the hall like someone had just fired the starting pistol in a hundred-yard dash. He was obviously out of bounds and facing a shot.

Similarly to the shakedowns, this often made me wonder, *If God called a lockdown census today, at this very moment, would we be out of bounds?* Are we indeed where God wants us to be? Or will we be like the guy running down the hall, trying to get where we know we are supposed to be, even though it's too late?

I mentioned earlier that the chaplain became a great mentor and friend. I started meeting with him weekly. He had a unique way of breaking down Scripture through a series of specific steps. He began teaching me how he prepared a message. His worksheet on immediate observations was my greatest challenge, and his greatest frustration with me. But I walked into his office one day after completing an assignment, and when he started reading, he got a big ol' grin on his face. He said, "I was just telling my wife I was out of ideas of how to get this concept across to you, and you just nailed it."

Sunday services were more like a traditional church service. We had a band formed from the inmates, and they predominantly sang hymns. We still used the 1980s hi-tech overhead projector for songs and sermon notes. We typically had around eighty men in attendance.

I have always wanted to return to Yankton and share the "dream again" message of hope, because I know precisely the hopelessness and shame the inmates are feeling. I understand because I sat in those exact same chairs! Just as I was wrapping up this book, I was invited and have now returned from preaching the Sunday chapel service. It brought back many memories, walking back into the prison camp. I wasn't exactly sure how I would be received, but God moved in an incredible way, and the comments from the men and the conversations with them afterward were remarkable. Taking our pain and using it to relate to others and speak into their life is what this is all about.

I received a note from an inmate after I returned home. A note like this makes it all worthwhile to encourage others:

> Everyone here was very grateful that you came and shared your testimony. It was encouraging on many levels. You have a unique experience to be able to share like you do. You really are fulfilling God's purpose for you by doing what you do. I pray that I will be able to do the same on my journey here and when I am released also. I will be here for a few more years, so I hope that maybe you will be able to come and share again sometime before I leave. Thanks for coming again.

My mornings in the study room were quiet times to be cherished. The only problem was that, over the course of time, men realized they could find me there and have a private conversation with me. Many a morning, they came and shared about issues they were facing—usually marital or family problems back on the home front. Even though it was interrupting my quiet time, it was an honor to be able to minister to these men at their time of need.

One of the tough things for me to understand initially was, "God, why did You even let the counseling center open? You know all things, and You knew I was going to be going away, so why did You risk the embarrassment to me, and more importantly, to the church?" Later, the answer became plain to me. God had two primary reasons for the center to open. His plans are always greater than ours. First, it gave me a much-needed landing and safe place after my release, plugging me right back into ministry where I had left off. And secondly, it never really closed; it just transferred locations to Yankton, South Dakota. The studies for my degree actually helped prepare me to be able to counsel other men better while I was in prison.

Yankton was actually a beautiful prison. It had buildings from the late 1890s and early 1900s. They offered a horticulture program, and in the spring, they planted nearly 240,000 different plants, roses, and flowers.

I was walking down the sidewalk one day, and there on a bench sat a man I hadn't met. Behind him were several rosebushes that must have had thirty to forty roses in full bloom. All of a sudden, I heard, "Hey, you!" The man's voice startled me, but I begin to walk over to him. He said, "We in prison." *Well, thanks for that wonderful reminder,* I thought. *I'm walking outside in the fresh air, trying to forget where I am.* "Did you ever, in your wildest dreams, think you would be in prison, and there would be roses in prison?" He went on, "We got roses, and we are in prison!"

I was still a little baffled at this sudden outburst, so I sat down to talk with him. His name was Brian, and he started telling me how he came from a medium-security prison, with triple-blade barbwire on top of a fence, and then another twenty yards away there was a second fence and more barbwire. There was very little grass, mainly gravel, and all kinds of crazy things that went on in the yard. He said some days when you looked at that bladed barbwire shining in the sun, the glare was so bad you needed sunglasses. "Yet here we sit in prison, no fences, green grass, trees, a nice bench to sit on, and we have roses!" When they first brought him to Yankton and pulled up in the bus, he told me he thought it was a joke: "This can't be a prison; they are just messing with me."

He said, "What I can't get over is all the negativity and complaining that goes on around here. In comparison to thousands of other prisons, this is like the Taj Mahal. But everyone is so focused on their prison that they miss seeing God's beauty."

I learned an invaluable lesson that day from Brian. Life can be tough; we can get so caught up in all our own issues and daily pressures to survive that we lose sight of God.

We become so consumed by focusing on the trial we are experiencing that it becomes our prison. All we can see is the fence (our problems) boxing us in. We miss seeing God's beauty, God's hand at work.

I believe that one of the keys to dreaming again is summed up in that phrase we have heard so often that it has become a cliché: sometimes, we just need to slow down and smell the roses. To change our perspective, to see that even though we are facing a major trial, God is still in control. Most inmates could only see the limitations of where they were—in a prison—and they totally missed enjoying God's beauty. They missed seeing God's hand still covering them and protecting them.

So, pause for a moment, reflect on the areas where God is blessing you, and recognize that the answer to your prayer may never look like you think it will.

One of the greatest blessings in prison was time. I was not happy about the amount of time I was away from my family in prison. Yet time slowed everything down. Gone were all the distractions this world can bring, all the problems we face at work and at home. In my opinion, one of the greatest attacks of the Enemy—and possibly one of the least recognized ones—is busyness. We become so busy with work, family, kids sports, school, and so on, that we rarely have time to slow things down. Prison showed me the power and importance of taking a sabbatical from time to time to be quiet and listen to God.

Several years ago, I was speaking to a friend of mine who had done some time as well, and he said something very interesting: "I never want to go back to prison, but I miss how simple life was there and how easy it was to hear from God."

In the midst of the trials and wars David faced, he always found time to reflect on God's goodness as a source of renewing his strength:

I will remember the deeds of the Lord;
> yes, I will remember your wonders of old.
I will ponder all your work,
> and meditate on your mighty deeds.
Your way, O God, is holy.
> What god is great like our God?

(Psalm 77:11–13)

CHAPTER 23

Takotsubo Strikes Again

I WAS NEARING MY HALFWAY POINT. I had settled into my comfortable daily routines, just doing my time. But special days and holidays could turn my mood in a hurry. August 16 was our twenty-fourth anniversary. I missed my wife and family so much, and this was a tough day to be without her. No one can comprehend what those words really mean when you state your vows: "For better or worse." The wedding day is a fairy tale and a beautiful day, which it should be. But soon life happens, tragedy strikes, and your vows are tested beyond your comprehension.

I sat in prison, reflecting on so much of our life. From the tough times of dealing with my wife's pregnancies, to surviving the loss of our son, to the numerous other things we had faced and conquered. I also reflected on my deep love for her and our unwavering commitment to make our marriage work, no matter what we encountered.

There is little doubt that we had drifted. That we had lost sight of our first love with all the trauma and heartache we had faced, and as the pressure of the legal issues pushed me back into a shell. We were nowhere near a divorce, but our first love was hidden underneath our broken hearts. But this separation began to draw us back to the heart of our commitment to each other, to reflect on our first love, to lean on each other for strength, and in the end, we would come through this stronger than ever. I was now faced with spending my twenty-fourth anniversary without the love of my life, but our commitment was unwavering.

My mood was starting to improve after our anniversary. I was trying to stay optimistic about the future, but one week later, I was hit with some gut-wrenching news that blindsided me once again.

Mitch Caster was one of Landon's best friends; they had met while they were both playing baseball with the Wichita Cardinals when they were twelve. Mitch went on to have a tremendous high school career in baseball and eventually signed with Wichita State University. His freshman year at college, my wife and I surprised him and showed up for his game unannounced. Though he had no idea we were coming, after the game, he showed us what he wore every time he played: basketball shorts with the panther paw and number 33, in honor of Landon, his friend. It meant so much to us. It's a blessing when you see people remembering your loved one.

There were so many others who did similar things. Trenton was Landon's first best friend from preschool and so like him in many ways. When we showed up to his football game unexpected, some of Landon's friends hollered at Trenton to come over and show us what was underneath his shoulder pads. There was a T-shirt with the panther paw and number 33. Brenden, a very close friend and neighbor, who spent endless hours together, used Landon's number on his race car to honor his friend, and when the river was rising with the potential to reach Landon's gravesite, Brenden went out in the middle of the night to save a bat, glove, and some balls that had been placed by his grave years ago. Priceless to have people still remember him.

Clint, another great friend and sports buddy, got married, had a son, and then called and asked us if it was all right to name his son after Landon. Andy was a preschool friend and classmate in the Christian school he and Landon attended together; many years later, Andy's mother would tell us that he named his son after Landon too. There have been so many great things done to honor our son that I hesitated mentioning any of them, because I knew I would unintentionally leave some other great friends out. We are so grateful to so many great friends who have walked out the hard road with us.

Each of these friends of Landon's were precious to us. So when we received terrible news about one of them, it broke our hearts all over again. Mitch was coming home from Minnesota where he was playing in a summer league and preparing for his senior year at WSU. He came into college as an outfielder, but with his 95-plus mph fastball, they were beginning to focus more on his pitching potential. He had spent the summer working on that part of his game, and it was starting to draw interest from professional scouts. Anyone throwing that hard will definitely get some looks. Many were beginning to think he would get drafted as a project, based on his arm strength. But while he was driving home from summer league, takotsubo struck again, Mitch was killed in a vehicle accident in Iowa.

My son sent me an email with the news that I read first thing in the morning, and I immediately called my wife and, while weeping, confirmed the tragic news. I went back and just sat on my bunk. I was in complete disbelief; tears were streaming down my face. It just had to be a mistake. *There's just no way this can be true.* I usually did my best to hide my tears in prison, but there was nowhere I could go to protect the sudden flood of emotion. Mitch was like a son to us.

I flashed back to a text I had received from Mitch before I left for prison, saying that he was so sorry for our family and what we were going through, that we had already been through so much, and he wished me the best of luck.

Mitch was a sensitive young man. A few months after Landon's passing, he and his dad came to see the Panthers,

Landon's basketball team that I was still coaching, play. He came to sit by us in the bleachers before the game, and all he could do was cry. There were no words; he was still flooded with emotions from the friend he had lost.

The last baseball game Landon played was with Mitch. We were meeting his dad, Mike, on a Sunday evening in Hutchinson after Mitch had spent the weekend with us. While his dad and I were standing by our cars, shooting the breeze, Landon and Mitch did what they typically did and started a hotly contested game of Wiffle ball. Those two were so competitive; during their games, they could argue like none about every strike and every foul ball and yet walk off the field as best friends, only to do it again another day.

Mike and I stood there laughing at the two. "They're two peas in a pod," he said. Little did we know, that would be Landon's last baseball game.

Now, upon receiving such heartbreaking news, I felt helpless. I wanted to be there for the Caster family. But here I was in Yankton, in prison, and I had limited phone minutes.

I went to the chaplain to get some counsel; I needed someone to talk to. *This can't be happening; someone, please wake me up from this nightmare again. First Landon, and now Mitch?*

I wrote from prison to the Facebook support page:

> My heart is crushed and goes out to the Caster family, who is one of the finest families I have ever met. The heartache and the grief they are feeling right now are beyond words. I have been able to talk and email with Mike, Mitch's dad, several times since the accident. Casters have been blessed with a wonderful memorial service for Mitch at the WSU baseball field and so many people that surrounded them to give them support during this difficult and trying time.
>
> I ask that you all keep the Casters in your prayers.

For his twin sister and his oldest sister. The journey down this path of losing a loved one is endless, but with the help of our Lord and prayers of friends and family, they will make it through this challenging process and journey.

I write this email in honor of a very special young man that made a huge impact on my life, and the life of my family, Mitch Caster. I will never forget you; my family and I will forever miss you and Landon! Two peas in a pod. Thanks for the wonderful memories.

Takotsubo had struck again.

CHAPTER 24

The Lonely Holidays

THE FALL PASSED BY QUICKLY, and it was nearing time for the dreaded winter weather in Yankton and facing the lonely, depressing holidays. Cold weather, limited time outside, and the approaching holidays spent without loved ones brought a different mood to the entire camp. A quiet heaviness and uneasiness were settling in all around us. Confined to the dorm and our work area, I felt myself wanting to slip back into the hopeless depression. The loss of Mitch, the weariness of this journey, the longing to be home, were overwhelming. I had to stay focused on the endgame. I was nearing less than ninety days until my release—or shall I say, I only had about thirteen more hamburgers to eat. I knew I had to finish strong.

I had been working hard on finishing my master's degree in Christian counseling and was nearing the completion. The closer the days were getting to facing my new reality, the more the old way of thinking was bantering with me. The Enemy was whispering, "You just wasted your time on that degree, you are a felon, nobody is going to want you leading in their church, no one is going to want to come and get any counsel from a failure like you. Are you going to give them advice on how to do things wrong?"

The Enemy will never stop whispering, never stop reminding us of our failures and the labels attached to them. I had to make a decision to either wallow in the potential unknown future or trust that God still had a plan for my life—like the day He spoke to me in my office: "If I got you from point A to B, can't you trust Me for point C?" I have thought about that statement often through the years, and I had to rest assured that the next stop in my journey was already taken care of.

I have described visitation feeling like Christmas morning, as I anticipated seeing my family. Now, when the real Christmas arrived, I woke up feeling almost paralyzed, with no motivation to get up and move. I just wanted to lie in bed amid the never-ending ache, longing to be reunited with my family. My thoughts drifted to wondering what my family was doing at that moment, reflecting back on my last Christmas with my mother, the first one without Landon, and now another busted special day that was meant for the celebration of Christ's birth and bringing families together. I lay there and thought, *Only eleven more hamburgers to go—just eleven; I am getting so close.*

I called my family and waded through the remainder of the day, trying to put my focus back on finishing strong.

I had two goals when I came into Yankton: to grow spiritually and to shrink physically. I felt I had accomplished both. I finished my master's degree. I had spent many hours with the chaplain, as he spoke life to me, and many an hour sitting in the study room, reading and growing spiritually. By the end of my sentence, I would walk out of camp having lost 115 pounds. I had grown and shrunk. I was ready for a fresh start!

CHAPTER 25

The Greatest Hamburger Ever!

I DEFINITELY LOVE A GOOD HAMBURGER, and I love trying every local burger joint I come across, but let's be real for a moment: the greatest hamburger I ever ate came from prison—clearly number one on my list! My last hamburger came on Wednesday, March 10; I was released the very next morning.

The day finally arrived; I was actually eating my final hamburger! I had started with forty-five to eat, and now this was it. Wow, did I enjoy and cherish every last bite of that amazing hamburger, and even though it was my last, it was still piled high with condiments! My countdown was finished, I had made it, freedom was just around the corner.

Now, the question was if I could get any sleep, given my anticipation for the next day. I finally dozed off sometime early in the morning, only to hear my alarm go off just after I'd gotten into a deep sleep. Wide awake immediately, I jumped out of bed and got dressed. I walked around to say my last goodbyes and headed toward the meeting point. I stood near the exit door, anxiously waiting for the officer to escort me to the warden's office to sign my release paperwork and get what money I had in my account. When the officer opened that door, I was primed, as if for a hundred-yard dash! But the officer escorting me clearly did not get the memo and was walking at a very casual pace. I thought, *If we can't run, can't we at least walk fast? Let's go!*

It was a picturesque, sunshiny morning when we began heading up the hill toward the warden's office. I glanced over my shoulder to the west, and there she was: my beautiful wife was standing by our car in anticipation of my release. Her love and support through the past year was the compass that kept me on track, that gave me hope that we were going to make it through together.

I signed my release paperwork and started the downhill walk toward freedom. We came to the edge of the property, and I couldn't wait any longer. I took off to hug my wife! What a glorious day, what a memorable hug. It's a shame that it is so easy to take things like a hug from a loved one for granted until they are taken away. God had blessed me with a wife who was not to be taken for granted but cherished.

Because I was still technically a prisoner of the BOP (Bureau of Prisons), I was not allowed to drive our vehicle. My wife had to drive me back to Wichita and check me in at the halfway house within eight hours of me leaving Yankton. Once I checked in, I was supposed to get released immediately for home confinement.

Just riding in a car felt great. The feeling of freedom, the changing scenery, the window down with the wind blowing in my face. With God's and my family's help, I had made it.

We stopped at a convenience store on my way back home, and I asked my wife for the money because I could actually pay for something! In prison, everything was handled by your ID card or stamps. It was a big deal just to use money again.

Even though I did not get probation like we were praying for, God's favor was always at work in our lives. I was told I was the first person in Yankton to be released straight to home confinement in a new program, skipping the halfway house. The favor of God!

Because I was the first to be allowed to do this, there was confusion at the halfway house in how to handle me going straight home. I had no choice but to spend the night at the halfway house until this was resolved. I knew it would just be a night or two, but it was still a crushing blow to my eager expectations.

After one night in the halfway house, I spent the next day worrying, while they tried to figure out how to handle the paperwork and release me. I was finally released that evening to go home and resume a somewhat normal life while wearing an ankle bracelet and having to document where I was at all times. It was a pain, but it was far better than the alternative! I was with my family, the people I loved so much.

CHAPTER 26

Time Served

THE PASTOR AND THE BOARD AGREED to let me return to the counseling center and also do some maintenance and setup/teardown for events. They had discussed whether they wanted me to return immediately or wait for a period of time. I totally understood their concern at having a freshly released prisoner on staff. One board member finally said, "We've stood with Rick this long; why wouldn't we keep standing with him?" The board agreed unanimously, and they were very instrumental in helping me launch back into ministry.

I would have completely understood if they had distanced themselves from me or if they felt I needed more time before they brought me back. But they took a risk on me because they believed God had a call on my life. God surrounded me with great people who looked beyond my circumstances and believed in God's call on my life.

I walked back into the counseling center, to the very office where I had experienced such highs and lows. I remembered the first day I moved into the office and the joy I'd felt at being back in God's plan. The joy of counseling people and the sorrows of walking with them through their issues. Then, just a year before, I remembered standing at this same doorway after cleaning out my office, feeling broken and desolate, figuring my brief moment in the ministry was now over. I remember crying as I walked out that final time.

Yet here I stood at the same heavy metal door that had slammed shut as I walked away, its loud thud symbolizing to me the end of a dream; it was now an open door I was walking through with a fresh start. *My dream is still alive.*

I stared at the name on the door. "Dream Again" was my fresh reality. What I'd been through was just a bump in the road; God's plan for my life was still on track.

I woke up my first morning of work, and I was so ecstatic. I was actually going to work at the counseling center, something I believed never would happen again. I was only a few days out of prison, and God had a landing zone already prepared for me. I knew that many fellow inmates struggled to find a job and their place back in society, and here I was living the dream and feeling overwhelmed by God's blessings.

I still had six weeks of home confinement, and that meant I had to call from a landline when I left home and call from a landline when I arrived where I was going. I had to provide the halfway house a list, a week in advance, of where I was going to be and get their approval on my schedule. If the place didn't have a landline phone, I simply could not go there.

I had anticipated being out of Yankton in time to enjoy Darian's senior year of baseball. I was devastated when I learned I was not going to be allowed to go to his games because there was no landline at the ballparks that I could use to call in and verify my position. I had to sit miserably at home and wait for updates from my wife on each at bat. At least I was going to be released from home confinement in time to be able to see his final tournament and watch him in his last summer of ball.

He had hopes of playing in college. He debated about going to a junior college or playing somewhere else. After several visits, he decided to sign with Manhattan Christian.

But then that summer he injured his knee again and faced his fifth knee surgery. Reality sank in for him; it was time to give up on baseball.

The halfway house made surprise phone calls to make sure the men were where they said they were supposed to be. They tried one of those calls on a Sunday morning while I was at church. Once the church service starts, the phones aren't answered. That was a big no-no, and they gave me a stern warning that this was unacceptable. I had explained why the phones weren't answered during that time, and that hundreds of people could verify where I was. Still, I understood they had rules that I needed to follow, and they had to do it by the book equally for everyone, and that meant a random phone check. I asked them if, on Sundays, they could try to check in earlier. I had to sit by the phone in an office while the church service started, and once they made their verification call, then I could go into the service.

At last, I finished my six weeks of home confinement, the ankle bracelet was taken off, and I could move about freely. I was still on probation and could not leave the state without permission, and I will be paying restitution for the rest of my life, but this season was over, and the future was looking bright.

In the fall, there was an opportunity presented to us to partner with a church that was struggling in another town—First Assembly in Hutchinson. That congregation voted unanimously to become a satellite campus of Believers Tabernacle.

Pastor Marty had taken Believers Tabernacle from about thirty people to close to a thousand at this time. My good friends Pastor Kendall and Rosie Sheats had been there from early on; they were the first hire for Pastor Marty and played a big role in their church growth. Rosie had a real gift working with kids and a heart to help launch the Wichita Dream Center, an outreach ministry that used the church's space. Pastor Kendall was a great associate pastor who just loved people. He remains, to this day, a great friend and a true confidant. Kendall and Rosie were an integral part of the church's growth and, like Pastor Marty, had sacrificed much when they first took their positions.

Kendall and Rosie had been through their own storms and had taken a season away from the ministry. This was going to be a fresh start for them also and one that they dove into headfirst, with a great passion for the church and reaching out to the inner-city kids.

The Wichita Dream Center, at its peak, bussed in nearly three hundred kids a week, fed them a meal, and presented the gospel to them. It offered food and clothing to those in need, a street ministry, and other special events, like giving away over eight hundred bikes for Christmas.

Pastor Marty always believed in second chances and helping those in need, which drove his passion for the Dream Center. Over the years that translated into hiring multiple ministers, like myself, who were also looking for a fresh start and maybe a second chance.

With Believers in Wichita taking on a new campus, we began the search for a campus pastor at our new location. Pastor Kendall and Rosie both felt God was calling them in a new direction and made a difficult decision to leave the main campus that they had put so much heart and soul into helping rebuild to become the campus pastors in Hutchinson, our new satellite campus.

This meant that there was a staff opening at Believers, and shortly, I was offered Pastor Kendall's spot as an associate pastor. We think our dreams end because of something in our past. We believe God can never use us again, and here I was, less than nine months out of prison and being launched back into full-time ministry at a thriving church.

I never thought I'd dream again after the loss of my son, and I never thought I'd dream again after being sentenced to prison. It felt like the sentence of death to my dreams. But God's plans and ways are bigger than ours, and just as the heart of the gospel is the resurrection of Christ, He continues to resurrect our dreams, our lives, our families, our careers, and on and on. He is our resurrected King, the master of bringing dead things back to life.

There are things in our lives that we may look back at and feel they were a total waste of time in view of our calling, but God brings them together for His good. Close to twenty years of business experience gave me the gifts and abilities that were now being put to God's use. The pastor saw those gifts at work and moved me into an executive pastoral role where I started handling more administrative duties, as well as continuing with ministry and counseling.

I walked into that church many a day and just wanted to pinch myself to make sure it was real. Not only had God put me back into ministry, but he had put me in a thriving church that was growing and doing so much for the community through the Wichita Dream Center.

It had been a long grind for Pastor Marty while rebuilding Believers Tabernacle over the previous twelve years, and he was sensing some early signs of burnout. After a lengthy discussion with the board, nearly everyone agreed that he needed a sabbatical. He started making plans for it to begin in January of 2013. With me handling so many of the administrative matters and with a great staff in place, this was going to be a new chapter, as I became to be the temporary lead pastor for the next four months while he was away.

It was a challenging time, trying to keep my head above water while still learning a lot about ministry and handling more of the preaching role. After four months of being in over my head, I felt like I was the one who needed a sabbatical. But during his time away, Pastor Marty decided to resign, and in May of 2013, he made it official. There was no downtime in sight for me; I was launched into leading the church until a new pastor could be elected.

Many people asked me if I was going to apply for the new position, and in some ways, it might have made sense to do so, but I just knew it wasn't God's plan for me, so I never really gave it much thought. I did my best to hold things together until the new pastor came on board, and then I knew that I most likely would have to resign so he could bring his new staff in.

That year was a heavy load on me, with all the demands of leading the church, and the uncertainty of what the future held for me in ministry. Similar doubts that I had battled in the past arose again, and I started thinking, *When I have to resign at BT, who is really going to want me?* But I knew that the same God who had lifted me from the despair of prison to a position to serve Him had this under control.

By fall, the pastoral search team had narrowed down their candidates down to three, and by November, they had a top choice ready to vote on. They opted to get through the holiday season and then have the candidate try out in January. He preached the first Sunday of the new year and received 94 percent of the vote.

The new pastor was no stranger to me. He had been my wife's youth pastor in high school, and he and his wife had served as our wedding coordinators. When I was on staff at Valley Center as staff evangelist, he was on staff also as the youth pastor. We had not had much connection over the past ten years or so, but we did have a good history together and got along very well. Pastor Bobby Massey became a great friend and did not want me to resign but, rather, to remain on staff with him. It was a very smooth transition for most of the staff and for me.

CHAPTER 27

$887 Parking Spot

THE NEXT TWO YEARS FLEW BY, and I felt like I would be at Believers Tabernacle until I retired. I loved the church, the people, and the ministry. But in the spring of 2016, God started stirring my heart: "You have a testimony that needs to be shared to bring hope to so many people." I prayed and internally battled with what I was feeling. BT had played such a huge role in my life and ministry. I had become comfortable and felt blessed with where God had me.

The first Sunday in June, I was asked to preach on the topic of passion. This was like the icing on the cake; while preparing for the sermon, I was forced to look closer at my own passion and calling. I said to myself, *I'm going to preach and challenge others about finding their passion. But what is my passion? What is my calling? Is my calling shifting a little?* While preparing that message, all those questions were hitting me right at the heart. In between services the day I preached, Pastor Bobby found me and told me that was the best sermon he had ever heard me give. It wasn't because of my words or how I delivered it, but because it was so personal to me and God was dealing with me about a new direction. In preparing the message, I was coming face-to-face with what had been stirring in my heart. When I met with Pastor Bobby about a month later, to resign, he said he hated to see me go, but he had known on that Sunday in June that something had changed inside of me. One of Pastor Bobby's most exceptional traits is that he loves helping launch people into their calling. He had spent years running the Bible Institute in Valley Center, assisting young people in finding their passion and calling.

My opening illustration for that message in June was an illustration from Faithlife called "Parking Space" by Stephen N. Rummage:

> That little 9 X 20 ft. piece of real estate in the parking garage is getting more and more expensive. If you commute into downtown Chicago, your parking spot can cost an average of $332.00 per month. But that's a bargain compared to midtown Manhattan where the average parking space goes for as much as $887.80 each month...
>
> The most expensive parking space in the world, however, is the one you and I occupy when we stop making forward progress in our lives. Parking has become a metaphor for people who just stop living. They settle into a comfortable spot, feel they've learned all they need to know, and aren't willing to expend the energy to keep going and growing. They come to a complete stop, turn off the engine, and parallel park along life's scenic route.[12]

I knew deep down that I had settled into a comfortable parking position, but God saw my time at Believers Tabernacle as preparing me for His next phase. I had a message of hope that so many people need to hear.

Fear is often the greatest threat to our passion, because fear is always comparing and calculating the cost, and if the cost looks too high or risky, then fear stops us from moving.

In the church community, we often think of fear as a bad

---

12 Stephen N. Rummage, "Parking Space," Faithlife Sermons, August 2007, https://sermons.faithlife.com/sermons/30082-parking-space.

thing, but fear is also a gift from God. Fear keeps us from entering situations that may cause us harm. Fear keeps some of us from driving too fast because we are afraid of what may happen if we lose control. Fear keeps us from going into a bad neighborhood at night. Fear of falling keeps us cautious when standing on the edge of a cliff. There is value in fear making us wary and potentially protecting us from injury. In many ways, it can be looked at as a gift from God.

And yet, this very gift from God can also be the thing that prevents us from experiencing the next level in our relationship with Him. Fear now becomes the curse. Fear becomes the great victor over faith.

Betty Miller, in her blog post "Overcoming Fear So We Can Yield to the Call of God," says it this way:

> I too, was afraid to surrender and let God take charge of my life and tell me what to do as one of my fears was *"What if God asks me to go to the foreign field and serve Him and live in a mud hut."* I did not want to live in the foreign field. Another fear I had at the time was, *"What if He called me to live alone for the rest of my days."*[13]

In her book *Letters from My Father's Murderer: A Journey of Forgiveness*, Laurie Coombs writes:

> Here's the truth. Sometimes, we simply need to do it scared. Over and over at this time, well-meaning Christians told me to "follow peace." I wasn't to move forward if I didn't feel peace about taking a step. But the whole "follow peace" thing can be a ploy—shrouded in holy words—used by Satan to bind us and keep us

---

13 Betty Miller, "Overcoming Fear So We Can Yield to the Call of God," *Bible Answers for Daily Living* (blog), January 15, 2015, https://bettymillerblog.com/overcoming-fear-so-we-can-yield-to-the-call-of-god/.

from following God. Jesus calls us out of our comfort zones into places of discomfort. And in these areas, we're not going to feel peaceful all the time. Yes, there is the peace of God that surpasses all understanding and is available to believers at all times, but often our propensity to rely on ourselves and do things our own way hinders us from experiencing that peace, which means sometimes following Jesus feels a bit crazy. A bit unsettling. Oftentimes we will feel scared to do that which God calls us to do. But make no mistake—fear does not negate the call. Fear is simply a by-product of our desire to control. When following Jesus into our unknown, scary places, God doesn't usually clue us in on the big plan. And this can feel anything but peaceful at times. But still, we must move.[14]

"Sometimes we just need to do it scared" spoke loudly to me and kept spinning around in my head. It gave me the courage to take a leap of faith. If we always wait for the perfect feeling or calmness in our decision, we may miss an opportunity.

One of my fears I had was about leaving my wife at home with a job that required me to be gone almost every weekend and sometimes during the week. Dake was living in Kansas City, and Darian was in Denver. They both were married to incredible women—Dake to Kristi, and Darian to Taylor. These women had suffered their own takotsubo, with Kristi having lost a sister and Taylor losing her dad when she was twelve. Dake and Kristi have given us three amazing grandchildren, and Darian and Taylor are now planning to add more grandkids to our fold since she recently finished her RN schooling.

---

14 Laurie A. Coombs, *Letters from My Father's Murderer: A Journey of Forgiveness* (Grand Rapids: Kregel Publications, 2015), chap. 4, Google Books.

Within a month of each other, both couples moved back to Wichita, bringing great comfort to me in knowing that they would be around to watch their mother when I was out of town. God is always orchestrating things!

There were plenty of people who felt I was crazy for leaving a thriving church ministry and stepping into the unknown. The fact is, if we see everything about our next step and understand exactly how it will play out, then it becomes nothing more than a calculated decision; that isn't faith. Faith senses God is leading you in a new direction and is calling your name. Fear changes its role from an advocate of our safety to a threat stopping us from experiencing God's purpose in our life.

When I finally made that decision to move on, I knew that with just Sunday services to preach, I couldn't support my family. So, once again, I used something from my past. I decided to sell windows during the week and travel on weekends.

I resigned publicly in July of 2016. It was an emotional day, but I was trusting God for the next step. Within two hours of me posting something on Facebook about my resignation, I got a message from Dr. Billy Thomas, saying that we needed to talk.

Dr. Thomas was my camp counselor the last year I went to youth camp. He was a young, on-fire youth pastor/evangelist, and we had immediately hit it off and were now great friends. Over the course of time and life, we lost track of each other, but it was one of those friendships that could reconnect in a heartbeat.

We can get so consumed with worrying about tomorrow and how we will survive, it's easy to forget that God is much further ahead of us than we can even fathom. He's a lifetime ahead of us. While fear was trying to push me back from my purpose, God had already placed Billy in my life over thirty years beforehand, so that when God called me in this new direction and I needed a landing zone, God had him in a position to offer me a great opportunity. Pause and let that sink in: thirty years in advance, God was preparing the answer for me at this time in my life. The same could be said about my friendships with Pastor Billy, Pastor Marty, and then Pastor Bobby. The list could go on and on, with God's provision being played out years in advance.

My grandparents and my mother may have been gone, but, clearly, I was reaping the blessing of the prayers they and so many others had planted. You want to leave a legacy? Leave a legacy of prayers and a covering over your family and friends!

Billy Thomas is a great friend. He is also the senior director of US MAPS (Mission America Placement Services) and wanted me to join their team as a US missionary working with MAPS.

MAPS has three legs to its ministry:

1. RVers. These are retired men and women who still want to do something for the kingdom. They travel all through the US, helping build churches. Churches provide materials, and the RVers offer free labor, saving churches millions of dollars a year. This is a great ministry that lets people dream again and still do something for the kingdom!

2. Church Teams. This division helps organize congregational teams that want to go help another ministry for a few days or longer. They will help in the building or remodeling process, or they will participate in a ministry outreach with the church they are serving.

3. Missionary Associates. This is a short-term opportunity for people, especially younger people, to go and serve up to two years in a ministry capacity. This can change the trajectory of their entire lives.

Billy expressed to me that MAPS numbers had been declining and that we needed a massive push for more recruiting so the ministry could grow and move forward. I realized that my testimony would open doors and, therefore, give me a great platform to represent US MAPS. I could tell people about the opportunities and needs of this ministry and challenge people to dream again, to find their purpose in life. Even if they were retired, I could challenge them: "Let's pick up a hammer and help build the kingdom!" It was a match that only God could create. I am very passionate about MAPS. So many opportunities to serve!

When Billy called me to explain the position, my heart was racing with excitement about the opportunity to remain in full-time ministry. Then fear and anxiety tried to halt my jubilee and take control. I'm thought, *Billy probably has no clue about my past, and once he learns about it, it will be a deal killer.* Even though I had been out of prison for over five years and in the ministry, the old shame still tried to sneak back in. *He'll never want me when he knows the real story.* I said, "That sounds amazing, but I'm not sure you understand my full history," and I started laying it out for him, fully expecting it to end the offer.

Billy's a visionary, and in his years of ministry, he has seen God use many people like me. He said, "None of that is a big deal. I will go to bat for you, and we'll make this happen." I was very fortunate, in spite of what I had been through, to have great friends who believed in God's call on my life.

I needed to fill out an application, get references, go through several interviews, and attend a conference before I became an official missionary candidate. The training only takes place in September and March, so I had time to finish all of this before the March training.

Once I was a candidate, I then had a year to raise my budget to transition from a candidate to an appointed missionary, working full time.

In the meantime, I continued selling windows during the week and traveling every opportunity I got on the weekends to share my story. It was a season of feeling I was completely where God wanted me, and yet so much uncertainty lay in front of me.

One of the first people who reached out to me was a pastor that had been on staff at the church where I was raised. He had always been gracious and invited me to preach when I was a traveling evangelist. It had been years since we had visited, but Pastor Randy encouraged me in my new adventure and was the first to reach out and book a service with me. Another great friend had been put in place to encourage me at a crucial time.

I get a bit nervous when I'm around Pastor Randy because he does enjoy a good practical joke. Like the time he invited me, as a young traveling evangelist, to come to preach at a sectional youth retreat for him. Before the night's service, he brought me up front and showed me a box with a chain attached to a key on each side and a padlock in the middle. He said, "Just because what you are preaching is good, and that's what we see on the outside, doesn't necessarily mean that's what's on the inside of you. We are going to open up this box and find out what's on the inside."

I was thinking, *Okay, I can play along with this. Something is going to jump out of the box, or there will be something funny on the inside, and I'll jump and act scared for all the youth. I can put on a show for them and play along with their joke.*

Little did I know that when I grabbed the key connected to the box by a chain with my right hand and then I grabbed lock on the front of the box with my left hand, I had just connected a positive and a negative to a cattle prong on the inside! You don't have to be an electrician to understand what had just happened! They had a dial control on it, and it was on a lower setting, but it was still a shocking experience! I often jokingly tell people that I call that box my salvation tester. Because if you can grab hold of that and nothing bad comes out of your mouth, then you are saved!

I had the opportunity to preach for Pastor Randy that fall as I awaited for my missionary confirmation. It was the first time I was sharing my testimony outside of my church. That morning, before I went to the pulpit to preach, Pastor Randy had me come up in front of the church congregation, and he prayed over me for strength as I shared my story. He also briefly mentioned the loss of my son. My nervous emotions were in high gear.

What happened next caused me to really fight back the tears. I sat back down, and Pastor Randy's ten-year-old grandson, Justin Allan, was sitting beside me. Pastor Randy had only made a brief mention about my son in his prayer over me, but Justin was listening and sensitive enough that he picked up on it. As I sat there with my eyes closed, praying, I felt a hand tap me. I looked over to see his grandson, with tears in his eyes, looking at me. "I'm so sorry that you lost a son," he said. Tears immediately started flowing down my face at the sincerity and honesty of a child. I'm still in awe at his grasp of and sensitivity to my loss from a simple prayer. God is going to use that young man!

March finally arrived, and it was time to attend the missionary training and officially be recognized as a full-time candidate. This started my one-year timeline to get my full budget raised.

The night before I was to start my training, I was sitting in a motel room, reflecting on the past, and literally in awe of how God had directed my path and how I was starting this new adventure. While reflecting, I wrote a note on Facebook, with sincere gratitude for those who stood by me and believed in me:

Hard to believe that this day has finally arrived! Tomorrow starts the US Missions weeklong orientation! Blessed to have some amazing people that supported me in this journey!

Dr. Billy Thomas for giving me this incredible opportunity to work with this amazing ministry, US MAPS. You patiently walked me through the application process! I'm very excited about what the future holds and to have the opportunity to work with you, learn, and be challenged!

Dr. Terry Yancey, who is a good friend that never stopped believing in me (even when I was running from God's call, he continued to stop by my work and leave his card to let me know he was still thinking about me). You were very instrumental in helping me walk through the licensing reinstatement process and having the support of the district for this appointment.

Bobby Massey, a loyal friend who did nothing but encourage me to follow God's calling and to take this leap of faith. I learned so much from you during my time at Believers Tabernacle!

In spite of all I have been through, I am truly blessed to be surrounded by some great men of God, who believe in second chances.

Raising a monthly budget is never a fun task, but having a steady, constant income once it was raised, allowed me to remain in full-time ministry, working with MAPS during the week and traveling on Sundays to preach the "dream again" message and to promote MAPS.

The next year presented plenty of challenges in raising support, but I was also exposed to some incredible men of God who are serving so faithfully on the front lines in their communities. I had the opportunity to hear people's gut-wrenching stories about what they had been through and how the "dream again" message was so timely for them to restore hope and believe that God could use them.

In the fall of 2018, I was fully commissioned as a US missionary and begin working full time with MAPS. It had been such a long journey, but once again, God's plan was moving forward.

CHAPTER 28

Self-Surrender

M Y MOTHER WAS AN INCREDIBLE WOMAN OF faith, but she was not immune to the Enemy's attack of fear. The key is that she surrendered those fears to her faith in God's plan. She wrote in her journal:

> Rick is almost grown up. He'll be off to college next year, but we've always had such fun. It'll be hard for him, but he's mature, and with the Lord's help, he will make it. Shawnda is just at the age she needs a mom to share her life with. I want to see her gymnastics meets, hear her sing, watch her excel as God uses her. She's going to rely on the Lord. When it gets tough, He'll be there for her. Krista, she's just starting junior high, she has so much growing up to do, lots of hard places to go through. She's my baby; she'll probably need me the most.
>
> I want to see them graduate. See them get married and have grandkids. Lord, they need me. Then it dawns on me: "You don't get to call the shots. God is omnipotent, and He doesn't make mistakes."
>
> I praise God for a place in Him where the Spirit of anxiety gives way to a peace beyond human understanding, for a Rock that is higher than I.

To dream again means we first have to be willing to surrender. My mother surrendered her greatest fear—of the future for her husband and children without her—and let her faith in God give her peace that only God can provide.

In my opening chapter, I talked about my physical journey to self-surrender at Yankton, and how little I comprehended how that statement would foreshadow the spiritual journey to self-surrender I was about to endeavor.

It is easy to open up a negation with the Lord, instead of just surrendering. Our greatest obstacle to surrender is that we often approach it as a negotiation: *Lord, I am willing to give these things up, but I really need to hold on to these.* Negotiation only delays God's big plan for us.

It's not, *God, if You will get me through prison, then I will...*It was me finally saying, *God, here is my everything, all my hurts, all my pains, and all my questions. But if You can use the loss of my son for Your glory, I'll do whatever you ask. If You can use me right now, right here in prison, I'll do whatever You ask.*

I went through eighteen months of thinking I was living a life fully surrendered to God, but in reality, I was withholding a vital piece of God's plan for my life. Once I surrendered that, God began to reveal His plans for me.

What are you holding back from God? What place are you unwilling to go? What are you negotiating with God?

I found freedom in prison. That may sound like quite a contradiction. I found freedom because I finally understood what fully surrendering to God was. I didn't get to just partially surrender to the BOP. I didn't get to just show up for prison on Monday, Wednesday, and Friday, or whenever it was convenient for me. I didn't get to take weekend trips home. I was entirely at their mercy.

They offered me the choice to voluntarily surrender to Yankton. Isn't it interesting how we can use words that don't really mean what they say? Voluntarily surrender? Like I got in line to sign up for the privilege of voluntarily going to prison? It probably should have been more accurately stated this way: "I'm here for my involuntary voluntary surrender. I don't want to surrender myself to prison, but if I don't follow through, the consequences will be much worse." They would have issued a warrant and forced me to surrender. So was it really voluntary or were the threat of consequences my motivation?

The truth of the matter is that we can choose to voluntarily surrender our lives to Christ, because one day every knee will bow.

Many times, life is about control. Not necessarily in the derogatory manner of a mean, controlling type of a personality trait. But we all do our best to make everyday decisions that allow us to control the course of our lives. Many of us have probably also experienced some poor decisions that sent us spiraling out of control in the wrong direction. In such a situation, the harder we try to regain control, the more frustrated and hopeless we become.

Control is the enemy of faith, and they are always at war with each other. God is leading us to do something crazy—something outside our comfort zone—when He asks us to jump out in faith, and we literally have no control over what happens next. The picture of either sinking or swimming enters my mind. Just as faith and control are enemies, faith and surrender work hand in hand. Surrendering to God's plan and trusting Him with your future can be one of the most exciting and terrifying times. But He never fails, when we surrender control by having faith in Him.

As I've stated before, I had two choices: *Do I surrender—or do I surrender?* Do I surrender to God's will and His plan and trust Him with my future, or do I surrender to fear and all life's problems and simply give up?

It's interesting that "surrender" is actually a battle term. When an army loses to another, they are asked to surrender their weapons and submit to the winner taking control of their country. This means yielding to some other rule of thumb. In practical terms, surrendering our lives means we have lost our battle to be king of our own life. But in this case, when we surrender, it actually means we win!

You can be surrounded by an army and offered a chance to surrender and refuse to do so. The army will then try to crush you into submission against your will, by severe force. At that point, you will have to unwillingly obey their desires for you.

The Enemy doesn't care if we voluntarily surrender to God. He wants to defeat us at all cost. He wants to take control of our lives. The thing is, he hasn't sacrificed anything for us. He just wants to create a facade that looks like a great path full of fun and happiness.

Many young people have looked at drugs or alcohol as a way to escape or a way to have a good time. Others have searched for a spouse to make them happy. Some have used their careers to make themselves feel better. All of them are searching for that elusive joy that only comes from willingly giving up the one thing we are convinced can make us happy: control. We think if we can just control our lives and our situations, we can make things better. Instead, we need to surrender that control to Christ.

God will never force us to surrender to Him. God is love, and He wants us to surrender out of our desire to pursue a relationship with Him based upon mutual love.

To voluntarily surrender my life is to recognize that I need a Savior, that the control I desire will never fulfill me.

To continue to grow in Him means we will find varying levels of surrender throughout our lifetime. Many times, there will be things we did not realize we were even holding back.

All of these acts of surrender ultimately impact our relationship with God. Our initial surrender to the drawing of the Holy Spirit leads us to salvation, and we become children of God at salvation. But this is just the start. Without the process, there is so much we miss out on; we miss what it means to grow in our relationship with God as he transforms us. Along the way, He goes deeper and He reveals new things we are still holding onto and ask us to surrender those to Him, and with each part we surrender, we draw into a closer relationship with Him.

The goal of the Christian life can be summed up in Galatians 2:20: "I have been crucified with Christ. It is no longer I who live, but Christ who lives in me. And the life I now live in the flesh I live by faith in the Son of God, who loved me and gave himself for me." This is true surrender.

In his book *No Surrender: My Thirty-Year War*, Hiroo Onoda tells his intriguing story of being one of the last Japanese soldiers to surrender in World War II. Onoda had been stationed on Lubang island in the Philippines when it was taken over by US forces in February 1945. The members of his unit were either killed or captured, but Onoda and a few others managed to escape and hide deep in the jungle. All the others were eventually caught, but Onoda evaded capture for over twenty-nine years. That alone is an amazing feat. His motivation for not surrendering was his devout belief and training in the military and that he had been told never to surrender his post until he received a specific order to do so. In 1974, the Japanese government sent its commanding officer to Lubang to find and order Onoda to surrender. When he stepped out of the jungle, he did so in his full-dress uniform and sword, with his rifle still in operating condition.[15]

I read that story and thought about how many of us try to evade the surrender of our desires and flesh, just like Onoda eluded surrender. Our flesh is stubborn and wants to stay

15 Hiroo Onoda, *No Surrender: My Thirty-Year War*, trans. Charles S. Terry (Annapolis: Bluejacket Books, 1999).

in control. Even in our minds, we struggle with surrender. Why is that? Is it the fear that, if we surrender, God will call us to do something we do not want to do? Like becoming a missionary in the North Pole or the jungles of the Amazon? Better yet, will He ask us to give up certain activities we— or our flesh—enjoy? There are a hundred excuses we can manage to come up with for not surrendering to God, but in the end, our desire to stay in control only leads to more problems. That is our pride: we think *we* can handle and control our life efficiently.

1 Peter 5:6–10 says:

> Humble yourselves, therefore, under the mighty hand of God so that at the proper time he may exalt you, casting all your anxieties on him, because he cares for you. Be sober-minded; be watchful. Your adversary the devil prowls around like a roaring lion, seeking some- one to devour. Resist him, firm in your faith, knowing that the same kinds of suffering are being experienced by your brotherhood throughout the world. And after you have suffered a little while, the God of all grace, who has called you to his eternal glory in Christ, will himself restore, confirm, strengthen, and establish you.

Through counseling and pastoring, I have run across some horrific things people have had to endure in their life- time—gut-wrenching stores of physical and sexual abuse, alcoholic parents, a parent walking away, and the list could go on. These folks are clearly the victims in these cases. They had no choice but to submit to the other person's behaviors and were too young to fight back; they had no place to run.

My counseling professor Dr. Reiner once made the state- ment, "You have to own your pain." I thought, *What? Own your pain? Even when someone else is clearly at fault for a person's suffering?* That just didn't seem fair. *How is that even fair, God?* This thought began circling in my mind over and over. I had a difficult time grasping that statement, and its intended meaning. Why did the victim have to own pain, a pain that should most likely be dealt with by the other person asking for forgiveness, not the victim owning it?

Then the Spirit began to reveal the meaning to me. If you are a victim who is harboring unforgiveness and deep wounds from your horrific experiences, then the other person always owns you. You are always tossed and thrown by wild emotions when you see the abuser, or think about them and the horrific things they did. In such cases, they have typically become masters at manipulating situations in their interactions with you.

But here's the truth that was revealed to me: *if you don't own something, then it's not yours to give away.* I can't legally walk into your house and grab food out of your pantry to give to someone who is starving. Even if you have a pantry full of food and we just need a few items that you probably wouldn't even miss. It would still be me unlawfully giving something away.

The same principle applies to our spiritual and emotional wounds. If we don't own our hurts and wounds, then we can't give them away, and if we can't surrender them, then we have no choice but to continue to carry them with us, to let them sit on a pantry shelf and eventually rot. We have no say about them because we have no ownership. But when we own the food pantry, then we can choose to give away the food to someone who is hungry. It's remarkable what happens when we own our pain, because once we accept ownership of it, then we get to decide what to do with it. And the best option is to surrender our hurts and pains to God and let the healing process begin. In essence, we take ownership of that pain and then transfer that ownership (since we are the rightful owners) to God.

I think sometimes we misunderstand self-surrender as

just a onetime act. There are days when I still reflect on the past and what we have been through. There are still days the Enemy tries to bring up the hurts of the past, the takotsubo of losing our son.

I was in Phoenix recently with James and Letha, who have been in ministry for twenty years—the last thirteen of those years with an inner-city ministry in Cincinnati that reaches out to the homeless and prostitutes. They recently expanded the ministry to the inner city of Phoenix. I have great respect for their heart for people.

As they showed me the homeless areas that they minister in, I began sharing with them about the word "takotsubo." They told me of their own horrific losses:

> We came home from one of our street outreaches in the inner city to find our nineteen-year-old son dead in our basement, due to a gunshot wound to the stomach. To this day it's still a huge mystery just what happened in that basement! We must simply apply Proverbs 3:5–6 to our lives.
>
> When we lost our only son, we had two choices! We could quit the ministry, get mad at God, and run away from God (which, to be honest, we were tempted to do), or we could trust God, run to God, and continue to plant inner-city churches all over America. The latter is what we chose to do, thank God.

In my opinion, this is a great example of owning their pain, and then giving it to God.

One year later, their three-month-old grandson passed away, and James preached the funeral. Having grandchildren myself, I can't even imagine how he had the strength to do that. Two major losses in a year. He told me, "It's amazing the supernatural strength and peace that God will give His people when we choose to run to God and to trust Him with our greatest pain and our darkest hours!"

As we were sharing about both of our losses, I began to tell about my moment of "self-surrender"—my defining moment along the road. Letha looked at me and said, "We may have a defining moment, but we also have to learn daily to surrender that to God." A light bulb went off in my head, and I said, "You are right. Those past wounds, the anger, the unforgiveness, the broken heart from losing a child will often try to make a comeback, but daily we must surrender those to God, deny ourselves in our pain, and trust Him with our future as we follow Him!

Then Jesus told his disciples, "If anyone would come after me, let him deny himself and take up his cross and follow me. For whoever would save his life will lose it, but whoever loses his life for my sake will find it." (Matthew 16:24–25)

Unsurrendered items in our lives will always be roadblocks to our dreams.

CHAPTER 30

The Storm

THE DREAM BEGINS with the willful surrender of our pain and our plans, but the dream continues with us trusting God, even in the midst of the storm that is trying to derail our dreams.

Proverbs 3:5–6 says, "Trust in the LORD with all your heart, and do not lean on your own understanding. In all your ways acknowledge him, and he will make straight your paths."

The Enemy will not just sit back; he will intensify the storms that attempt to steal our dreams.

It was a cold day in late December. My wife's cousin Vance and I were hunting ducks at a lake in Kansas. It was cold enough that the lower end of the lake was frozen. We had scouted it out the day before and found the ducks and geese were using the ice as their roost. In addition, we knew that this part of the lake was protected from forecasted winds for the next morning.

We left our house around 4 a.m. in time to get to the lake, boat across the water, and set our decoys out before sunrise. The morning hunt started out great, and now, right after lunch, a flock of ducks came flying in. We knocked down a couple, but one we just crippled, so it was swimming away. Vance went to get the boat to go retrieve the duck. I stayed at our spot on the point. After a few minutes of not seeing him come around the corner in the boat, I went to check on him. He told me to go back out to the point and keep hunting as he changed the spark plug on the motor.

I hunted on the point for another thirty minutes and killed a few more ducks. Still not seeing Vance come around the cove in the boat, I figured something was wrong. Sure enough, he had not been able to fix the motor because the Ziploc bag holding the spare spark plug had gotten a hole in it and water was frozen to it. With the temperature below freezing and no way to melt the ice on the spark plug, we decided it was time to pack up and head to the truck.

This is where the story takes a scary twist. The wind shifted toward the end of our hunt, and now it was in our face as we headed back to the truck. With probably close to seven hundred pounds to carry, between us, the dog, and all our gear, it was going to be a long haul. All we had were two very short paddles, probably 4 feet long, and it was difficult to get a strong push with such small paddles. But we had no choice; that's all we had. The north side of this lake was completely vacant. No houses, no roads coming into it. We started paddling to the opposite shore, which seemed like miles away. What had started as a sunshiny, promising day had very quickly turned into a windy nightmare. Now the storm clouds were moving in, the temperature was dropping, and it was becoming darker and drearier by the minute.

If we stopped paddling to rest just for a moment, the wind pushed us back, and we quickly lost any ground we had gained. I don't scare or panic easily, but it started to feel like a hopeless situation, like we might never get to the other side before the storm front moved in.

I picked out a landmark and kept my eye on it, just to verify if we were actually moving toward the truck, because in the middle of a big lake, rowing against the waves, it's difficult to see any progress at all. The reality was crashing in with each wave that hit on the front of the boat. We hadn't seen another person on the lake all day. While we were frantically paddling, I saw a small plane fly overhead, heading west. I began to pray that they saw us and called the Park Rangers to come to check on us. I have no idea how long it took us to get to the other side; I'm guessing it was a couple of hours. We were drenched in sweat from head to toe, from sweating in our bulky clothing and from having to row for such a long period of time directly into the brutal wind, and we were completely exhausted. We both thanked the good Lord for giving us the strength to row nonstop.

I've often thought back to that day and compared it to the many storms in life I've faced. Our small rowboat might be heading across a vast opening on the lake of trials and tribulations, traveling directly into the wind, and it might feel like we are not nor cannot move forward. We are in a situation that we clearly aren't equipped for, and life feels like it is about to overwhelm us. Small boat, short oars, heavy load, heading directly into the storm, and no end in sight. Things are not looking good. It feels like each wave that is crashing against our life is just one thing after another attacking us, and it never stops. The perfect storm is attempting to take us out.

I wondered if my life was going to end that day. But adrenaline is an amazing thing, and we just kept focused on the task at hand—rowing.

The storms of life will try to kill our dreams. We will feel hopeless and overwhelmed at times, the storms we are facing are intimidating and powerful, and maybe one day we just lose sight of our dream and quit rowing. At those times, I wonder if we are even aware that we stopped rowing; we are just so exhausted from the fight. Then the wind takes command and blows us back into the vast hopelessness of lost dreams. Our dreams sink, our purpose is gone, and we walk numbly through life with no feeling of purpose.

Or we can choose to trust Christ to be our captain, to help us navigate through the storm.

You can trust God that He still has a plan for your life, that you can even dream again because He promised He would never leave us nor forsake us.

Big dreams, radical dreams, will often go against the wind and the world. These dreams may not be popular, they may not be the way we do things—*but God*.

There were many a day, I was ready to give up on my dreams and just quit because nothing was going as I had imagined it. It felt like life's hurts and decisions were going to sink me. If God wanted me back in the ministry, prison sure was a strange way to make that happen!

CHAPTER 31

Dream Again

I'M REMINDED OF THE STORY of Joseph in Genesis. What must have been going through his mind in a dark and dingy prison, betrayed by his family, with nothing to show for his life, except for a dream from God?

Even before Joseph's dream, his brother's animosity toward him was building. Genesis 37:4 says, "But when his brothers saw that their father loved him more than all his brothers, they hated him and could not speak peacefully to him."

Hatred was already prevalent among them, and then Joseph shared his dream. It probably wasn't the wisest thing for him to share this with his brothers—but he was just a naïve seventeen-year-old young man, excited about a dream God had given him. Maybe he thought that by sharing his dream it would make things better with his brothers; they would finally appreciate him and, more importantly, respect him!

> They said to one another, "Here comes this dreamer. Come now, let us kill him and throw him into one of the pits. Then we will say that a fierce animal has devoured him, and we will see what will become of his dreams." (37:19–20)

Unforgiveness, built on hatred, has no limits on the

depths we can fall.

There is little doubt that Joseph's brothers were jealous, and their jealously grew into hatred. They were jealous of the way their father favored him, and then to throw gasoline on the fire, they definitely were not happy about the idea that their little brother was going to be over them, according to his dream.

Why are we often threatened by someone's big dreams? Is jealousy at the heart of it? Are we possibly jealous that we don't have the guts to step out in faith and pursue our dreams? Are we jealous of their blessings? Do we ever wonder, *Why them, Lord, and not me?*

His brothers were discussing ways to kill him, and in essence, kill the dream. It's interesting that they say, "And we will see what will become of his dreams." They were obviously very threatened by his dream. They eventually decide that, rather than kill him, they would simply trade him to a caravan, accomplishing the same thing without getting blood on their hands. The dream would be dead when he was a slave.

Earlier, I shared about the bitter men I had met in prison, who had been abandoned. Can you even fathom the level of bitterness that tried to overtake Joseph? The reality that his own brothers had not just abandoned him in his time of need but had methodically planned out a way to get rid of him. It's hard enough being betrayed by a friend, but being betrayed by family is a whole new level.

Joseph found himself a slave in Potiphar's house. The dreamer, who was to be in a position of power, was relegated to slave.

But God's favor was upon him, and suddenly things were looking up again, and he was promoted rapidly. I'm guessing he was likely thinking that his dream had a real chance again; things were back on track. Maybe he thought, *Look at where God has placed me.* Surely the excitement was building within Joseph, while he faithfully served his current master. But then disaster struck again:

> The LORD was with Joseph, and he became a successful man, and he was in the house of his Egyptian master. His master saw that the LORD was with him and that the LORD caused all that he did to succeed in his hands. So Joseph found favor in his sight and attended him, and he made him overseer of his house and put him in charge of all that he had. From the time that he made him overseer in his house and over all that he had, the LORD blessed the Egyptian's house for Joseph's sake; the blessing of the LORD was on all that he had, in house and field. So he left all that he had in Joseph's charge, and because of him he had no concern about anything but the food he ate. (Genesis 39:2–6)

It is easy to see God's hand on Joseph. Then Potiphar's wife took notice of him, and when he refused her advances, she was furious and falsely accused him of taking advantage of her. Potiphar reacted like most men when it appears that our wife's honor is at stake. He responded quickly and harshly, driven by the anger of the betrayal from someone he trusted.

Joseph was sent to prison. Maybe now he thought, *Lord, if it wasn't hurtful enough that my own brothers betrayed me, if it wasn't harmful enough to be falsely accused of something I'd never even consider doing, now I am unjustly thrown into this dingy prison. I guess the dream is dead.*

I felt a similar feeling when the high of the counseling center opening was squashed by the reality of going to prison. Reality tries to tell us that there is nothing good that can come out of prison, and our dreams will never be fulfilled. I'm guessing that Joseph probably had similar attacks by the Enemy.

We have to hold tightly to two factors about dreams God places in our hearts. First, if it were easy, we could do it on our own, and we wouldn't need God. We wouldn't need to grow in faith for our calling. Second, we will most likely face times of opposition, unfair treatment, and discouragement. Times when we feel we are traveling down a dead-end road, with no room to turn around. I thought prison was the end of my dreams—but God! The more desperate and unlikely the situation, the bigger God shows up! *Never* let go of His promises!

We often feel stuck in a prison of unfulfilled dreams. For me, this was a literal prison. I knew God had a plan for my life, but being in prison and labeled a felon changed everything. Deep down, we know that God has called us to do something special, but what happens when every door and every attempt to launch into our purpose or calling is met with failure? Multiple failures turn into discouragement, and discouragement turns into hopelessness, and hopelessness turns into the wasteland of failed dreams, stacked on top of "what-ifs."

What if we become paralyzed, afraid to act or even think about a new step toward our dream because everything we have tried has failed, and we fear just another embarrassing failure. At such times, we learn to be comfortable in our prison of self-pity and eventually accept a purposeless life.

What if Joseph had given up after betrayal and his heartbreaking setbacks. The power of the what-ifs is that they generally tend to keep us looking backward, unable to move forward. What if I had just folded with my dream of the counseling center when I was heading to prison? I sure felt like it, but if I ultimately had, I wouldn't be where I am today; I wouldn't be sharing this message of hope and faith. Our trials and our what-ifs become our testimony to encourage others that if God helped us through it, He will help them through their trial also!

There comes a tipping point. A point where we either decide to stay in the valley of bitterness and defeat, or we reach out in faith for what appears to be an elusive promise that God's Word has given us. The dreams He has laid on our hearts are often given to us to help us to see beyond the storm. We are forced to say, *Okay, God, You have shown me Your plan, You have given me a promise, and I will stand on that promise.* Staying focused on that can help propel us out of our dungeon of despair.

Even in prison, God was at work. God wasn't caught off guard. The favor of God was with Joseph, even in what appeared to be a devastating setback, a setback that at the time looked to be fatal to the dream he had. In reality, it was all part of God's plan. Never underestimate the favor of God and His sovereignty to use our trials and tribulations for His glory, as the foundation for our dreams!

> But the LORD was with Joseph and showed him stead-fast love and gave him favor in the sight of the keeper of the prison. And the keeper of the prison put Joseph in charge of all the prisoners who were in the prison. Whatever was done there, he was the one who did it. The keeper of the prison paid no attention to anything that was in Joseph's charge, because the LORD was with him. And whatever he did, the LORD made it succeed. (Genesis 39:21–23)

Eventually, the Lord opened the door for Joseph to interpret a dream for the Pharaoh. Almost overnight, out of nowhere, he went from prison to the palace. He was promoted from the prison of unfulfilled dreams to dreaming again.

Why is it so hard for us to understand, in the midst of

a trial, that God thrives in taking our mistakes and using them for His glory, in breaking all the odds? Our mistakes can bring shame and embarrassment and regret to us personally. All we can see are our imperfections and failures, but God sees a vessel to be used. It's our failures that truly show God's grace.

My wife usually bakes and decorates her own cakes for all the family birthdays. Years ago, she was pulling my birthday cake out of the oven and noticed that the middle had caved in. Being a perfectionist, she figured this meant she had to start all over again.

My wife is also very creative and resourceful, and she began to think about the design of the cake. She decided that, instead of making a brand-new cake, to simply use the imperfection as part of the design of the cake. She would make it look like this was how she planned it all along.

She was making me a golf cake, to look like an actual fairway, complete with a golfing figure standing on the tee box. But instead of scrapping the whole cake, she saw a way to use the indention to make it look like a sand trap. But then she faced another obstacle. It would have been easy to create the sand trap with brown sugar, but she was completely out. She thought about her options and came up with a mixture of sugar and cinnamon that made a tremendous-looking sand trap. When I first saw the cake, I had no idea of the backstory. I had no idea the cake was ruined, by many standards; I saw a golf cake, and I loved it. Then she explained to me what had happened, and it had even more meaning to me.

My wife used the imperfection to make a special cake for me—one that I will always remember.

Isn't that a great picture of what God does with us? We make a mistake, or we've made poor choices, leaving us scarred, and we want to throw the cake away and start all over. We think, *God if I could just begin this life all over again, I would certainly do things differently.* I can assure you, I've thought about that multiple times. *If I could just start over.*

Yet we miss the whole point of what beauty really is. Why is the golf cake my all-time favorite cake, and I still talk about it thirty years later? Because it took the imperfections and turned them into a strength that only added beauty and realism to the cake.

I wish I remembered every cake my wife has made for me, but truth be told, I have forgotten many of them. But not the golf cake. What makes our life memorable and an inspiration to others is to see our imperfections and mistakes, and to see how God has used them for his glory!

I still fight the feelings of being like that collapsed cake: *I'm going to carry around this tag "felon" for the rest of my life. People will look at me and see my label, and who wants a "felon" counseling in their church or leading their church?*

Instead of this downward spiral, I can choose to view things from God's perspective and realize that these events in my life have given me new insight and a much deeper compassion for people than I ever knew before. I can relate to them and understand their hurts at an entirely different level. My imperfections and failures have allowed me to become a much more effective counselor, pastor, father, husband, and friend.

I had a gentleman approach me at the altar one time, and he said, "How do you do that? How do you stand up there and share your failures? I was labeled a felon from an incident shortly after high school, and I'm always afraid to tell anyone, but you stood up there and openly shared about your mistake."

I get it. I fully understand what he was saying, but there came a point in my life when I realized that my past opened new doors for me to do ministry. When others hear about my failures and brokenness, it allows them to open up to me and potentially see how God can use them, just like He is using me. A broken vessel, saved by grace

To never understand our purpose in life is a heavy burden to carry. We were all specially designed, using all our imperfections and mistakes to fulfill God's call. If God can use me for His glory, then He can take anyone and use them for His glory! Our life story is a powerful testament to God's plan in all our lives!

I firmly believe that every person in this life has a purpose—whether it is leading a church, leading a life group, serving at a food distribution, quietly cleaning up after an event, or joining US MAPS and helping build the kingdom. God always has a purpose for your life—big or seemingly small—but, in God's sight, there is no big or small. It takes everyone to make the church function. Everyone, every role, is vitally and equally important!

Closing

M Y PRAYER FOR THIS BOOK is that by being open and honest—about the questions I had about God, my pain of losing my mother and a son, my failures and the embarrassment of going to prison—it may inspire you to find God's purpose for your life, to "dream again." To realize everything in our lives is an opportunity for God to get glory.

My mother loved God; she loved life, loved to laugh, and loved to play jokes. But more than that, she loved people. She used laughter to brighten someone's day, but she was also super sensitive to people's needs and bringing hope into their lives. My cousin Cheri shared of her generosity:

> Aunt Connie was selling gold jewelry, and I had just turned sixteen, and she gave me a gold ring with two amethyst stones and a diamond. She shared how much she loved me and that I was to wear the ring with honor and to keep myself pure. I wore that ring with so much pride. Aunt Connie taught me to be the "fun" aunt… the "crazy" aunt…the "loving" aunt. She always made us feel so special.
>
> Connie understood compassion and friendship at the deepest levels. She was my camp counselor and would hold me tight at night when I was a child and would get homesick. She was my mother's best friend. My mom and her had so much fun, and they were not only sis-

ters-in-law but best friends. My mother still talks about how great of a friend Aunt Connie was to her.

I'm going to close with another excerpt from my mother's journal. We all face tough times, we all battle moments of doubt, and we all have a story. But if we will just trust God and stand firm, He will never fail us. Even though my mom passed, I can still see her confident smile and hear her voice speaking these words to me: "Don't be moved. Trust God. He will take care of you!"

She writes, exhorting herself:

> Cancer may seem like a big thing to you, but the way you handle the little things will determine how you handle the big things. If you buckle every time someone offends you or every time you have a marital spat or kids disappoint you, you'll never make it through the big things. We have to determine not to be moved by these things.

She continues writing,

> I came home from the hospital on Sunday, and the next Sunday I went to church in the evening, and I thought, *This is ridiculous. There's no reason for me to be sitting out here*, so I told the music director that I wanted to play again. I could've waited out two or three months and let Satan sit back beside me each service and talk to me, making it harder and harder to start playing again, but I determined I was not going to be moved. I was going to continue to serve the Lord in the same capacity. The longer you procrastinate, the harder it is to do what you should.

The picture of my mother sitting at the piano, worshipping God, while carrying her portable oxygen tank is an example of a faith that is in action and not moved. Although life was dealing her a severe blow, she never lost her laughter, and she never lost her faith. The greatest lessons she left for us kids were actually found in watching how she handled adversity.

As Christians, too many times we want God to do all the work. We don't want to have to make a decision; we think salvation is God waving a magic wand and living in the land of "everything is roses"—as long as we serve Him, everything will be peaches and cream. Why, then, did God spend so much time in the Bible telling us how He would lift us up, how He would not let us be tried beyond what we could bear? If there would be no problems, He could have saved a lot of ink and just said, "Accept Me."

But the Scripture says, in 1 Peter 1:6–7, "In this you rejoice, though now for a little while, if necessary, you have been grieved by various trials, so that the tested genuineness of your faith—more precious than gold that perishes though it is tested by fire—may be found to result in praise and glory and honor at the revelation of Jesus Christ."

Fire only separates all the foreign, impure materials from gold. It loses nothing of its nature, weight, color, or any other property; genuine faith will only be proved by trials.

I mean this was from the Lord, because I was so overwhelmed; if we could just learn to turn to the Lord for communion and fellowship with Him when life and circumstances overwhelm us!

But too many times we want to try to handle it ourselves, or find a sympathizer, or ask, *Why me, Lord?* Instead, we make a real mess out of it. David says, "When my heart is overwhelmed, lead me to the rock that is higher than I."

She continues,

> At this point, I just began to pour myself out before the Lord, to commune with God as a friend. Psalm 62:2 says, "He only is my rock and my salvation, my defense and my strong tower; I will not be shaken or disheartened" (AMP).
>
> I claim that I shall not be greatly moved. You know what that doesn't say? It doesn't say that God is going to zap you, and you will be suddenly steadfast. That statement is an act of faith and your will to stand on that promise, when David declares, "I shall not be greatly moved." We have to make a decision: Am I going to drift whichever way the wind blows? Whichever way circumstances take me? Or am I going say with David, "I shall not be moved!"?

Some might say that my mother's passing should have affected my faith and planted some doubt about God. And for years, I did allow that to happen. I questioned why God didn't heal such an incredible woman, full of laughter, full of faith. I viewed her death more from the perspective that God had failed us.

Then I realized the greatest lesson my mother left for her family was actually her last act of faith. Her greatest example of faith was seen in her final moments in her battle with cancer and ultimately her death. Because she never wavered, she never moved. Her faith wasn't based upon whether God healed her or not, her faith was based upon what was finalized on the cross with Christ's resurrection and defeating sin. She genuinely trusted God with all her heart. She passed away, but she was not moved! What an incredible legacy she actually left—a woman of true, unmovable faith.

Dream big dreams and have the faith not to be moved when the Enemy tries to derail those dreams! Our dreams aren't based upon just a miracle; our dreams are based on what Christ accomplished on the cross, and He will never fail us when we keep it in that perspective. The greatest gift you can leave your family is the gift like my mother left us, one I did not recognize for many years. Leave your family and friends a legacy of what unmovable faith looks like, to never give up on the dream God plants in your heart. That's a true legacy! Dream again!

Order Information

To order additional copies of this book, please visit
www.redemption-press.com.
Also available on Amazon.com and BarnesandNoble.com
Or by calling toll free 1-844-2REDEEM.